The Dividing Discipline

The Dividing Discipline

Hegemony and Diversity in International Theory

K. J. Holsti
University of British Columbia

Boston
ALLEN & UNWIN
London   Sydney

Allen & Unwin, Inc.,
Fifty Cross Street, Winchester, Mass. 01890, USA

George Allen & Unwin (Publishers) Ltd,
40 Museum Street, London WC1A 1LU, UK

George Allen & Unwin (Publishers) Ltd,
Park Lane, Hemel Hempstead, Herts HP2 4TE, UK

George Allen & Unwin Australia Pty Ltd,
8 Napier Street, North Sydney, NSW 2060, Australia

First published in 1985

Library of Congress Cataloging in Publication Data

Holsti, K. J. (Kalevi Jaakko), 1935-
   The dividing discipline.
Bibliography: p.
Includes Index.
1. International relations—Research.   I. Title.
JX1291.H65   1985   327'.072   84-24270
ISBN 0-04-327077-8 (alk. paper)

British Library Cataloguing in Publication Data

Holsti, K. J.
   The dividing discipline : hegemony and diversity
in international theory.
1. International relations
I. Title
327.1'01   JX1395
ISBN 0-04-327077-8

Set in 10 on 11½ point Palatino by MCS Ltd, Salisbury, Wiltshire
Printed in Great Britain by Billing & Sons Ltd., Worcester

Contents

Introduction

This essay examines the state of theory about international politics. It focuses on (1) the major substantive debates that presently engage scholars who ponder the condition of our world, and (2) some characteristics of the academic discipline: Who produces the significant work? Is there a global community of scholars, intellectually and temperamentally equipped to take a genuinely universal perspective on international politics? What are the elements of hegemony and pluralism in the theoretical organization of the field? I start from the position that since the middle of the seventeenth century, when the states system of Europe was being organized, there has been a single paradigm that has guided thinking in the field. That paradigm, in which the world is portrayed as an anarchy (meaning political fragmentation), with no overarching authority to organize the fundamental activities of the essential constituents—the nation states—has sustained a long tradition of philosophical and empirical work which has had as its core concern explaining why and how nation states go to war, conduct their diplomacy, construct institutions or customs leading to peace, order, and stability, and how they organize power in pursuit of their objectives. The major insights of Hobbes, Grotius, Rousseau, Morgenthau, Bull, Deutsch, and many others have all been developed within this paradigm. Some commentators have emphasized the differences between these figures, outlining the contours of different "schools" or approaches. I emphasize the commonalities because I am convinced that all have been concerned with essentially the same intellectual questions, no matter what their unique perspectives and answers. Thus, until recently there has been an intellectual hegemony in the sense that a single paradigm has served as the theoretical platform of our field. This hegemony is not necessarily to be lamented, provided that critical questions generated by the paradigm meet certain tests, including isomorphism, logical consistency, the capacity to generate research, and reasonable correspondence with the observed facts of international politics.

Theoretical pluralism—the development of new or competing

paradigms—is to be applauded only where previous formulations are fundamentally flawed in one or more domains, or where *established* international trends and events render them obsolete. There is no automatic virtue in paradigmatic pluralism, as there might be in political faiths. The hegemony of the nation-state system paradigm (here called the classical tradition) may help contribute to our descriptive and explanatory storehouse of knowledge of international politics, while new departures or challenges may lead us to intellectual dead-ends, including the investigation of trivia that have no long-range intellectual payoff. On the other hand, if the classical tradition *is* seriously flawed, then new departures may help us redirect inquiry into the proper channels. A third alternative is that new theoretical formulations may be synthesized with, or grafted on to, the classical tradition. Cumulation would imply modest rectification and/or blending, but not replacement. The succeeding chapters will describe two bona fide challengers to the classical tradition—dependency theory and global society theories—and assess the extent to which they are taking root as the intellectual guideposts of both empirical and theoretical work in international politics. They will also evaluate the possibilities for synthesis. Or must one ultimately supplant the others?

The problem of *what* kind of theories we use to understand and explain the world of international politics is not divorced from *who* does the theorizing. How we see the things in international life that intrigue or depress us depends to a certain extent on our geographical vantage point. No matter how we try to compensate for our cultural biases we can never "know" the real world in its entirety. We will have biases, priorities, and prejudices that are deeply ingrained by our education, national culture, diplomatic history, and the daily headlines—all of which typically express national rather than global perspectives. The various streams of theoretical activity undertaken within the classical tradition deeply reflect the historical experience of the European states system in the past, and the cold war more recently. It would be perfectly legitimate, therefore, for an Indian or African scholar to claim that other historical experiences should help form the basis of theories about contemporary international politics.

Within the classical tradition, such national and limited-historical perspectives have been prominent. Almost all of what we call international theory today has been developed by observers from only two countries, Great Britain and the United

States. Important exceptions exist, of course, but this essay will demonstrate that there is as yet no international community of scholars in the field. There is only an Anglo-American core of "producers" with small appendages in other anglophone countries, Japan, Scandinavia, and Europe. As international relations develops into an academic discipline globally, will lasting theoretical contributions come from a variety of national academic groups, or will the Anglo-American hegemony continue into the indefinite future? The second purpose of the essay is to locate and measure the degree of pluralism in the production and consumption of theoretical knowledge in international politics.

In writing this type of essay, the author always has in the back of his mind a specific audience. As a teacher of introductory and advanced courses in international politics and international theory, I have had to face the problems occasioned by theoretical debates, the blossoming of "new" approaches, and the proliferation of specializations, journals, research communications, jargon, and the like. A teacher in our field increasingly has to make critical choices in selecting materials for students. Given the time constraints of most courses, he or she can no longer hope to provide a genuinely comprehensive offering, including a reasonable introduction to the competing paradigms and the kinds of research they have spawned. If one is going to make rational choices in material selection, some explicit sets of priorities must be developed for guidance. In my view, no such guidelines exist today. A third purpose of the essay is thus to enhance awareness of the problems surrounding intellectual hegemony and pluralism, and to help the reader in coming to his or her own conclusions about priorities and perspectives on the world.

I do not provide answers, although I do outline my own biases and preferences. Many will disagree with them, and if so, I will have accomplished the purpose of making readers sit down and think through what it is about international politics they want to emphasize, why, and if possible, to come to some conclusions about the long-range value of the competing paradigms. If the teacher or graduate student has to contemplate the problems raised in the essay, his or her students will probably benefit in future in terms of increased course coherence, and enhanced appreciation of the intellectual roots of our discipline. To the extent that active research programs are articulated more carefully and their unexplored assumptions or hidden normative purposes come to see the light of day, the essay will have garnered an additional bonus. I do not preach consensus, but urge those in our field to understand exactly where they are intellectually, and why they are there.

The research and writing took place under the auspices of one of the great fringe benefits of academia, the sabbatical. The locales were ideal. Professor J. D. B. Miller invited me to spend three months as a Visiting Fellow in the Department of International Relations, Research School of Pacific Studies, at the Australian National University. A department of distinguished and intellectually lively people, combined with strong library facilities, provided an excellent venue for the research part of this work. I am also grateful to Professor and Mrs Miller for numerous kindnesses of a nonacademic sort. I wrote the manuscript in a small house, in the town of Mithymna, on the island of Lesvos in Greece. No further comment is required, although I would like to express my thanks to two close friends, Dr Andreas Psomas and Professor Dimitri Constas, both of Athens, who helped in numerous ways. The project was made possible by funding from the Social Sciences and Humanities Research Council of Canada, the Izaak Walton Killam Memorial Fund for Advanced Studies at the University of British Columbia, and the Social Sciences and Humanities Research Committee of the university. I am deeply grateful that in a time of serious academic retrenchment, research of this kind can continue unimpeded. I am also indebted to Alexander George, Denis Stairs, and Mark Zacher, all of whom supported my applications for the research grants.

Four graduate students did exceptionally fine work in helping to generate the data for Chapters 5 and 6: Vidya Nadkarni and Syed Ahsan of the Department of Political Science, University of British Columbia, Noh Seung-Joom of Yonsei University, Seoul, and Yamada Takahiro of Sophia University in Tokyo. Ole R. Holsti, Michael M'Gonigle, and Vidya Nadkarni read the entire manuscript and made numerous helpful suggestions. I am always impressed how persons with busy agendas are willing to take the time and trouble to improve their colleagues' efforts. I have not heeded all their suggestions, but overall, the book's merits are based on this assistance.

Dory Urbano and Izabela Sobieska did all the typing, no easy feat considering the state of my manuscripts.

K. J. HOLSTI
Vancouver
October 1983

1

Hegemony and Challenge in International Theory

Everywhere, it seems, established patterns [in world politics] have either come to an end or been greatly modified. (Rosenau 1980, 13)

We are now in an era without a paradigm to provide a framework for questions we ask ... or [for] answers we expect to find sufficient as explanations. (Morse 1976, xvi–xvii)

International theory is in a state of disarray. In the past decade, the three-centuries-long intellectual consensus which organized philosophical speculation, guided empirical research, and provided at least hypothetical answers to the critical questions about international politics has broken down. New conceptions and images of the world, and how it works in the diplomatic, military, and commercial domains, have arisen. Scholars have offered trenchant criticisms of the "realist" tradition, which goes back to Hobbes and Rousseau, severely challenging the assumptions and world views upon which it is based. Some have outlined alternatives, not so much because they promise better understanding through methodological innovation, but because they are supposedly more consistent with contemporary realities. The continued underdevelopment of many new states, combined with the startling pace of technological transformation, have raised new kinds of questions about international politics, questions which were not relevant to the kinds of problems contemplated by our intellectual ancestors and most of those working within the realist, or classical, tradition.

1

The "behavioral revolution" has had little to do with the present debates. In fact, one could write at the end of the 1960s that all was well on the international theory front, once the vigorous quarrels between methodologists had subsided. Researchers had, after all, isolated key areas of inquiry—areas which had commanded considerable attention from the philosophers of the eighteenth and nineteenth centuries. These were no less than the causes of war and the conditions of peace. But disillusionment with "grand theory," overarching statements about the fundamental (and recurring) structures and processes of international politics, had suggested that greater rewards could be reaped by focusing on more discrete phenomena—alliances, power, integration, and the like—in the hopes that "islands of theory" would eventually emerge (Holsti 1971). Research, whether quantitative, ideographic, philosophical-historical, or comparative, seemed to be concentrating on the critical questions. The linkage between theory and research programs was secure: each fed upon the other.

Today, no such sense of well-being or satisfaction exists. There is no longer a consensus on the subjects of inquiry and theorizing. The view that international theory should be organized around the structures and processes of the states system, the activities of the great powers and their decision-makers, particularly as they relate to war and peace, is no longer accepted by a significant number of scholars. Newer theoretical variations propose different problematics,[1] and entirely different conceptualizations of the world. The thrust of the new work has centered on "grand theory" and the ultimate philosophical problems of a discipline: How should we look at the universe we wish to describe and explain? Are our models of international politics reasonably consistent with realities? Who are the significant actors and units of analysis in international politics? Should we continue to ignore economic processes and actors? Do fundamental economic structures, on a global scale, determine the main outlines of states' external policies? What are the critical normative problems in the field? Indeed, some have asked whether it is possible to generate reliable knowledge of present realities if the assumptions we have held as self-evident for more than three hundred years no longer hold. Do we really want to study alliances, integration, decision-making, and the rest when critical questions about the continuing relevance of traditional concepts such as power and the states system need to be raised first?

Before examining the dimensions and character of the new theoretical activity, we should first delineate the boundaries of the field, international theory. By this field, I mean descriptive and explanatory statements about the structure, units, and processes of international politics that transcend time, location, and personality. This is a crude definition, but it helps exclude from the discussion the thousands of books and articles that deal with discrete phenomena and events. Grotius and Hedley Bull are theorists of international politics because they advance descriptive generalizations about the sources of war and the comparative effectiveness of various norms, procedures, and institutions in muting international conflict and establishing order and stability. Their purpose is to discover commonalities, central tendencies, or essential characteristics of states in their international behavior. To the extent that their analyses also account for the genesis, change, or termination of war, or the network of norms, institutions, and procedures in the states system they move from description to explanation. Similarly, Rousseau and J. David Singer are theorists because they are commonly concerned with the sources of crises and wars, across time and space.

Robert Keohane and Joseph Nye were among the first[2] to criticize the classical paradigm for ignoring transnational processes and nonstate actors. By locating new agents of action and their mutual relations, they vastly expanded the boundaries of the field. And in proposing that issues other than war/peace/security/order should command attention, they challenged a consensus among international theorists that stretched from Hobbes and Rousseau to Ernst Haas and Raymond Aron.[3] But while Keohane and Nye wanted basically to add the possible influence of nonstate actors to more traditional conceptions of international politics, subsequent critics have taken a further step by claiming that the whole nation-state paradigm is fundamentally unsound and inadequately consistent with present-day realities. It is not just a question of adding new types of actors to analyses, but of reconceptualizing both actors and processes in international life. For example, in 1974 Donald Puchala and Stuart Fagan argued that the "prevailing security politics paradigm has become overly restrictive," and that "a number of us ... sense that international politics have changed structurally, procedurally, and substantively in the last ten years" (Puchala and Fagan 1974, 249). Edward Morse's view, quoted at the opening of this chapter, provides an even more critical stance, echoed in Rosenau's claim that the "conduct of foreign relations and the course of international affairs seem so different from the past as to justify an assumption of fundamental structural change" (Rosenau 1980, 83).

The works culled for these quotations represent only a sample of the recent critical literature in international theory. There is much more evidence of theoretical ferment in the field. Academic journals such as *International Organization* have been recast to include many articles dealing with new types of phenomena in international politics, new perspectives on old problems, and extensive analyses of concepts such as international regimes (a new idea, perhaps, but one with strong roots in the Grotian tradition). Several important collections of essays appeared in England[4] during the 1970s, offering arguments supporting the continuing relevance of the classical paradigm, or extolling the virtues of newer perspectives, such as dependency theory. In North America almost every academic conference and journal in the field has had sessions or articles devoted to new conceptions of a "global society," or to dependency studies where exchange, exploitation, world capitalist system, and center and periphery replace the language of traditional international theory. To summarize the competing claims for theoretical novelty or primacy, anthologies such as Maghroori and Ramberg's *Globalism versus Realism: International Relations' Third Debate* (1982) have appeared. That title suggests that the sides are drawn up, the issues neatly dichotomized, and as in the Realism versus Idealism, and Traditionalism versus Behavioralism debates of the 1950s and 1960s, one side is likely to emerge victorious.

Consequences of Theoretical Profusion: Dialogue or Confusion?

But the debate cannot be simply between two sides; and it is not merely a question of which picture or model of the world is more consistent with realities. More fundamental questions are involved; they concern questions of the appropiate or crucial units of analysis, of the core and peripheries of the field, and most important, of the proper subject of study. The stakes in the debate are immense: if the debates lead to an authoritative outcome or consensus, the research agenda of the future may change profoundly.

4

Can a debate be conducted when we are not certain whom to include among the participants? Globalism versus Realism suggests only a single cleavage in international theory, while most who have tried to classify the various schools or paradigms in the field come up with at least three categories, and often more. A brief review of some of the efforts to create taxonomies of contemporary international theory reveals the considerable theoretical confusion that reigns today, making it difficult to organize a coherent debate, much less a dialogue leading to constructive synthesis or to the emergence of a "super paradigm" that will once again authoritatively guide inquiry, help organize research agendas, be substantively accurate, and provide criteria for developing reading lists for undergraduate and graduate students.

Contemporary writers in international theory do not agree on the means of classifying the contending approaches: each uses somewhat different criteria so that we do not have even a roster of schools, persuasions, or paradigms. Ralph Pettman suggests that today there are two main paradigms, the pluralist and the structuralist. These correspond roughly with the traditional state-centric international politics model, with a multitude of states of unequal capabilities, each pursuing its perceived national interests, and often engaging in war. A structuralist perspective, on the other hand, "confronts global politics in terms of the horizontally arranged hierarchies that run across geographical boundaries, throwing into high relief the patterns whereby 'overdeveloped' states reproduce characteristic socio-economic and political forms within the underdeveloped ones in terms of the uneven spread of the industrial mode of production, the uneven and complex character of the class systems that have grown up in its wake, and the current global division of labour" (Pettman 1979, 53–4). But Peter Willetts suggests that there are really *three* paradigms commanding attention in international theory: the realist, which is the traditional state-centric model; the functionalist, which employs models characterized by a multiplicity of actor types and issue areas (with corresponding variations in typical behavior); and the Marxist, the major concern of which is the origins, character, and consequences of economic exchange in a world capitalist system (Willetts 1981, 100). Christopher Mitchell likewise formulates a triad of contending schools, but his differs from Willetts's. Behavioralism, which in his view has been confined largely to North America, is predominant, followed by traditionalism, a preserve of British academics, and the Marxist approach, which has been most influential in West Germany and Scandinavia, drawing its inspiration from the Frankfurt School that rejects the positivist philosophy guiding behavioral research (Mitchell 1980, 43–4). Rosenau also outlines three "major approaches to world politics" (state-centric, multi-centric, and global-centric) but his categories are based on criteria different from those used by Pettman, Willetts and Mitchell (Maghroori and Ramberg 1982, Foreword).

With a better sense of the historical antecedents of contemporary international theory and with an appropriate scepticism regarding the contention that every innovative "paradigm" is really new, Martin Wight outlined *four* main traditions in the field, each of which is based on a different model of the world: Hobbesian anarchy; a global community of mankind, following the Stoic, Roman, and medieval Christian traditions; a Kantian model of world society; and the traditional Grotian notion of a society of states (Wight 1966, 38). Hugh Collins (1982) has also defined four theoretical "clusters" in the field. And so the list of taxonomies goes on, to a record of twenty-four types of theory that Kulbakova and Cruickshank identify in their own classification (1980, 273). Such numbers suggest substantial confusion in the field, lack of a commanding methodology, and no uniform philosophical basis for academic inquiry.

If, as Arend Lijphart has claimed (1974, 49), a single image of the world, or paradigm—defined as a model or vision from which springs a "coherent tradition . . . of scientific research"—unified the field until the advent of behavioralism, then clearly we have seen a significant change. We now appear to have many traditions, but it is not easy to tell how many because commentators cannot agree upon the criteria to use in making the critical distinctions between them. Rosenau, for example, uses a single criterion, the main units of analysis; but Mitchell employs a combination of methodological, geographical, and philosophy of science underpinnings, implying that these will determine what we see and what we want to study. Collins is on safer ground with his notion of clusters, because he comes close to defining approaches or schools in terms of the *object or subject of study*. But despite this merit, his taxonomy cannot be compared to Pettman's because the latter employs a broad criterion, types of essential actors in the system, to distinguish between schools.

Thus, who will participate in the debate? How many will be

6

invited? Can all "realists" really be lumped into a single Hobbesian tradition, particularly when some of Hobbes's ideas on international politics have been misunderstood? Can a member of a Marxist school or approach speak on behalf of a global-centric model of the world? In some ways, the answer is yes, but non-Marxist globalists would probably prefer to speak for themselves. Is an advocate of the study of transnational relations really speaking on behalf of a competing paradigm?

As succeeding chapters will try to demonstrate, there is not much chance of achieving an authoritative outcome of *any* debate. But in an attempt to create a little more order out of the confusion that presently reigns, let me propose three criteria for distinguishing among genuine paradigms. They have little to do with methodologies or conceptual tinkering. They are ultimately important because they help identify the *subject matter* of international theory. To develop theory, before we can discuss technique, there must be some consensus on what we want to examine. This is the heart of the matter. Such a consensus has reigned in the field until very recently. Hence, we can talk of a classical tradition. The serious challenges today come not from those who want to add or subtract types of "essential" actors, or those who argue that not all of international politics can be characterized as a "struggle for power." The most serious onslaught against the classical tradition comes from those who would change the core subjects of the field. This is essentially a normative rather than scientific question.

Guidelines to Inquiry in the Classical Tradition

Rousseau and Morgenthau, Hobbes and Bull, Bentham and Haas disagree on a number of matters; but they are also joined by a common set of questions or problems that, implicitly or explicitly, establish the boundaries as well as the core of the field. International theory has traditionally revolved around three key questions, the first of which is absolutely essential, the raison d'être of the field, with the other two providing the location for solutions to the problem. While the criteria are not easily delineated, with some overlap between them and some conceptual fuzziness at the edges, they have provided the guidelines for more than three hundred years of inquiry in the field. They are:

(1) the causes of war and the conditions of peace/security/ order; an essential subsidiary problem is the nature of power;

(2) the essential actors and/or units of analysis;

(3) images of the world/system/society of states.

The first question (or criterion for a taxonomy of approaches in the field) provides the rationale for the study of international politics. While some may argue that we have organized a field called international relations/politics because the phenomena are "there," the truth is that we study them because of a deeply held normative concern about the problem of war. Virtually every writer who has helped develop the field has been animated by this concern, including Hobbes, Grotius, Erasmus, Vattel, Saint-Pierre, Rousseau, Kant, and all the moderns. Each has made some sort of implicit or explicit statement about the causes of war and, perhaps more prolifically, has proposed some sort of solution to the problem (although Rousseau, having made his proposal, rejected it as impractical). Why this concern? Most nineteenth- and twentieth-century authors have lamented the human and institutional costs of war—lives lost, destruction of productive facilities, moral degeneration, and political upheaval. With the advent of nuclear weapons the problematic becomes even more compelling. It is *the* problem of universal import. But it was not always so.

For example, Greek and Roman writers pictured war as a normal activity of political communities, ever present and always to be anticipated rather than prevented. Some German and English writers of the nineteenth century, and some writing in the Marxist tradition, have portrayed war as a progressive motor of history, an opportunity for proletarian revolution, or a device for weeding out the unfit and weak. But for the rest, from Hobbes and Grotius to the moderns, war is the problem to be analyzed, and at least equal energy must be devoted to outlining avenues of escape from this endemic problem, whether through a confederation of states, international integration, disarmament, foolproof deterrence, or some combination of them.

War is also the central concern of international theory because it has been a major source of historical change, a profound determinant of *all* political life. To quote Hedley Bull,

> war appears as a basic determinant of the shape the
> system assumes at any one time. It is war and the

threat of war that help to determine whether particular states survive or are eliminated, whether they rise or decline, whether their frontiers remain the same or are changed, whether the people are ruled by one government or another ... [and] whether there is a balance of power ... or one state becomes preponderant. War and the threat of war ... are so basic that even the terms we use to describe the system—great powers and small powers, alliances and spheres of influence, balances of power and hegemony—are scarcely intelligible except in relation to war and the threat of war. (Bull 1977, 186)

Thus, the essential behavior to be described and explained in international theory is that which relates to peace and war. Subquestions explore problems of security, order, and power. To Aron (1966) and most others writing in the field, this is *diplomatic-strategic* behavior, which has a domain of its own and is distinguishable from domestic politics—and we might add, international economics—because it operates under the constant backdrop of organized violence. While the intertwining of domestic and external, and commercial and diplomatic concerns has become particularly pronounced in the last few decades, this does not nullify the traditional observation that there are fundamental differences between diplomatic-strategic behavior and the activities of politicians and traders at the local and international levels.

The second criterion, the units of analysis and/or nature of the essential actors, was more often assumed than explored in the classical literature. Nation states are the essential actors, not only because they share the legal attribute of sovereignty and because many norms and practices are designed to protect their independence, but because they are the actors that *engage in war and are essential in organizing the norms and institutions which provide more or less stability, security, order, and/or peace for the system.* Since the decline of the papacy in secular affairs, no actor other than states could create peace and stability; and none, with a few exceptions such as pirates, could make war. Since the 1950s, the state as actor has been disaggregated to the extent that decision-makers and bureaucratic organizations have accounted for specific actions. But there has never been any question that these individuals or groups are agents of the state. They act as trustees of the national interest.

The third criterion—world images—is also important in help-ing us to distinguish among the current contenders for theoretical primacy. The argument is whether to characterize the world in terms of a society of states, a global community of individuals, a universal system of capitalist exchange, or a hodgepodge of citizens, transnational organizations, bureau-cratic interests, supranational institutions, and the like.

Most writers of the classical tradition, including the moderns, have had little problem with this issue. International theory properly focuses on the consequences of a world made up of sovereign states, each possessing the capacity to make war against the other, and all suffering in various degrees from the security dilemma. The logical consequence of this image is, to use Stanley Hoffmann's phrase, "the state of war."[5] This has provided the protagonists within the classical tradition a major debating point: Is war the only, or even the major consequence of the system? To pessimists such as Rousseau, it was; observers in the Grotian tradition have emphasized instead the possi-bilities of complementary interests, the relevance of norms in restraining behavior, and in Bull's terms, the important muting elements of "society" in the system of states. While war and peace, or the conditions for security and order have been the major problems, modern writers have extended the area of study to include all those forms of behavior, short of war, that also follow logically from a system of states, including such phenomena as the sources and nature of power, diplomacy, bargaining, crisis behavior, and deterrence (cf. Clark 1980, 19). This work has been undertaken within the classical paradigm.

To recapitulate, until recently the major contributions to inter-national theory occurred within a single paradigm. Despite numerous debates and disagreements, there has been a funda-mental consensus on these three questions: (1) that the proper focus of the study is the causes of war and the conditions of peace/security/order; (2) that the main units of analysis are the diplomatic-military behaviors of the only essential actors, nation states; and (3) that states operate in a system characterized by anarchy, the lack of central authority.

The Hegemony of the Classical Tradition

The term paradigm, like "discount prices," "classic," and "national liberation," has been stripped of much meaning by those who claim for their innovations a certain novelty. To have one's own paradigm may be helpful for academic advancement or notoriety, but the claim cannot be honored unless the innovations offer *essential differences* of theoretical perspective, not just additions, or deletions from established problematics and world views.[6] I believe the three criteria outlined above are sufficient, and probably necessary, to distinguish between genuine paradigms in our field. If so, we can legitimately claim that the main figures in the classical tradition have operated within a single paradigm, and that their modern successors have only expanded, but not altered the fundamental features, of that paradigm.

Until the outburst of theoretical activity in the 1970s, the international politics, state-centric paradigm, which I will call the classical tradition, provided the intellectual framework for all facets of academic international relations: theorizing, the development of normative positions and policy preferences, empirical research on a vast range of questions, textbook-writing, and teaching. Although some zealous behavioralists dismissed the works of the founding fathers as "impressionistic" or "non-scientific,"[7] the fact remains that the debates of our field's historical figures have heavily influenced modern research agendas, as we will seek to demonstrate in the next chapter.

The current debates are fundamental. The real challenges to the hegemony of the classical tradition come not from marginal additions or deletions (in Rosenau's term, "meddling"), such as acknowledging the importance of some nonstate actors, disaggregating the field in terms of issue areas, or focusing on crises rather than wars; they come, rather, from new and entirely different conceptualizations of the priority problems within the field, and from fundamentally different ideas about the appropriate units of analysis, the important processes, and the kind of context in which actions and processes take place.

The only two challenges which, according to the three criteria, qualify as separate paradigms are (1) world or global society models and, to put them together, (2) dependency/world capitalist-system theories.

There are of course many different versions of these two paradigms. The debates among the *dependencia* theorists, as well as the world capitalist-system advocates, are furious and probably interminable. There are numerous branches and perspectives among the global society theorists as well, even if their debates tend to be somewhat more muted. But like the different schools within the classical tradition, all the contending factions within each of the challenging paradigms adhere to common views regarding the three criteria. Since our purpose is to examine these challengers only in terms of their relationship to the development of international theory, we will not explore their internal debates.

How serious are these challenges? The second part of this volume will present some evidence to analyze this question. Here, it is sufficient to note that class reading lists, some textbooks, and numerous publications, both in journals and as books, propound the virtues of the new paradigms. Large research programmes on dependency have been organized, not only in Latin America, the original home of dependency theory, but also in Europe and North America. An American research organization honoring one of France's leading historians, Fernand Braudel, serves as the home of Immanuel Wallerstein, who has contributed so much to conceptualizing the image of a world capitalist system. Terms such as compradour bourgeoisie, the global commons, center and periphery, and international feudal hierarchies fill the pages of numerous international relations conference papers. This is not the vocabulary of the classical tradition. There are, then, grounds for believing that the challenges to the classical hegemony are not mere fads, to pass away under the influence of the next cold war crisis which should reestablish the paramountcy of traditional international politics. We are witnessing a true struggle over paradigms, over intellectual priorities in terms of theory development, and for future research agendas. Our tasks in the succeeding chapters will be to demonstrate how and why these challenges are so important, to explore the possibilities for synthesis with the classical tradition, and to assess the desirability of such a synthesis. Or, as some suggest, perhaps there should be a wholesale abandonment of the classical tradition. Should we then search for an entirely new theoretical foundation to guide future work in international politics?

A National Academic Hegemony

The classical tradition represents not only a type of intellectual hegemony; it is also a national academic hegemony—or at least an oligopoly. In the twentieth century, most of the theoretical work in international politics has been done by English and Americans, with several contributions from other predominately English-speaking countries such as Australia and Canada. A few essential works have also come from continental Europe. A discussion of the state of international theory ought to include consideration of this fact for at least two reasons: (1) if the domain of international theory has been populated mostly by academics from several countries, is it not likely to be badly biased in its assumptions, models of the world, and prescriptions? and (2) is it really desirable, assuming the value of a genuine international community of scholars, to have just a few figures "producing" international theory? An ideal model of a community of scholars would suggest reasonably symmetrical flows of communication, with "exporters" of knowledge also being "importers" from other sources. This ideal model may find some degree of approximation among the research-oriented institutions of the Anglo-American academic scene in international relations (though probably not as symmetrical as one would find in some of the natural sciences); but if we look at the global collection—one hesitates to use the term community—of international relations scholars, the degree of asymmetry is so high as to constitute a virtual national academic hegemony. The purpose of the second part of the volume, then, is to offer a crude measure of the extent to which contemporary international theory constitutes both a paradigmatic and a national hegemony, and to look for evidence of diversity in both theory and scholarship.

But before we turn to these questions, it is necessary to provide some substantiation for the major assertions of this chapter concerning the continuity and hegemony of the classical tradition. In particular, to what extent have the three criteria been central to the thinking of major figures in the field? Has there in fact been a single paradigm which ties together both the classic figures and the moderns, including behaviorally oriented research?

Notes: Chapter 1

1 Some readers may be unfamiliar with this use of the word "problematic." It is a translation of the French noun *problematique* and was imported first by structural anthropologists, I believe. It refers to a subject area of study and the particular means of inquiry employed to analyze it.

2 A variety of Marxists, in positing classes rather than states as the critical

13

actors in international life, and in claiming the unity of domestic and foreign policy, really made the first concerted attacks on the classical paradigm of international politics. Historically this is accurate, but since international theory as part of a discipline has mostly ignored Marxist views of international life until recently, the Keohane-Nye volume represents an initial *systematic* critique of one of the main features of the classical paradigm; more implicit critiques are observed in nineteenth-century liberal thought and in the works of Karl Deutsch in the 1950s and 1960s. See the introductory and concluding essays in Keohane and Nye 1972.

3 This position was not, however, inconsistent with views expressed by Jeremy Bentham and some early nineteenth-century liberals. See below, pp. 28-9.

4 e.g. Donelan 1978; Kent and Nicholson 1980; Taylor 1978a. Australians have made significant contributions as well: see Pettman 1979 and Miller 1981. This list is illustrative, not exhaustive.

5 The most succinct analyses of the core ideas of the classical tradition remain Hoffmann 1965 and Waltz 1957.

6 There are numerous definitions of paradigms, but for our purposes the notion of their functions is most important. They are basically selecting devices which impose some sort of order and coherence on an infinite universe of facts and data which, by themselves, have no "meaning." C. R. Mitchell discusses some of these functions and suggests that paradigms "focus attention on a particular level of analysis, different units and unit attributes in order to explain a problem which is also, to some degree, determined by the paradigm" (Mitchell 1980, 40-1). While war and peace as the core subject derive from normative concerns, they also derive from the third criterion, the image of the system of states. Hence, the normative concern is a sufficient but not a necessary condition for international theory. But most peace plans which did not take into consideration the essential characteristics of the states system were doomed to failure. I realize this use of the term paradigm is somewhat narrower than the meaning developed by Thomas Kuhn in his seminal *The Structure of Scientific Revolutions* (1962). To him, paradigms are rooted not just in rationally analyzable differences, but in trans-rational perceptions, or gestalts.

7 For example, the comment by J. David Singer, "How much longer will we believe that if one person *thinks* such and such is true, that this constitutes useful knowledge" (italics in original), quoted in Rosenau 1980, 209 n. 16.

2

The Continuity of the Classical Tradition

> Whoever studies contemporary international relations
> cannot but hear, behind the clash of interests and
> ideologies, a kind of permanent dialogue between
> Rousseau and Kant. (Hoffmann 1965, 86)

International relations as an organized academic discipline is
young compared to most areas of social inquiry. Systematic
thought regarding the activities of independent political units is
of course much older: Thucydides is often cited these days as
among the first to derive generalizations about the behavior of
city states in war and peace. Kautilya in his *Arthashastra*, written
during the Mauryan dynasty, also made observations that
transcended the critical issues of the times, although his purpose was to advise statesmen, not to develop a field of study.

In the formative years of the European states system, it was
mostly philosophers who, in the context of their more general
works, contemplated aspects of international relations. Among
them, Rousseau and Kant devoted specific treatises to elabor-
ating plans for peace. Most of the lasting work in the nineteenth
century was the product of English philosophers, particularly
the liberal descendants of Jeremy Bentham.

By the early twentieth century, specialists in international
relations and law had found institutional settings in universities
and some foundations, and were thus able to devote their full
energies to the analysis of diplomatic affairs. The disciplinary
roots of these specialists were predominately history and law,
although a few had come up through new departments of
government and had considerable familiarity with the works of
the great Western political philosophers. In England, specialists

in international relations had somewhat broader classical training and possessed particular interests in and talents for analyzing the writings of the classical tradition's founding fathers. This commitment to the study of the intellectual heritage of international theory continues to be a characteristic of British scholarship, in contrast to that of the United States. Outside the Anglo-American world, international relations as an academic discipline did not come into existence until the post World War II years, although there were numerous European and Japanese experts in such specialities as diplomatic history, international law, military studies, and international organizations in the 1920s and 1930s.

The field of international theory, as it developed in the university setting in the early twentieth century, had a strong normative element bequeathed from nineteenth-century English liberalism. Works that offered generalizations often manifested assumptions and views such as the inherently pacific nature of democracies compared to despotisms, the restraining effects of public opinion on foreign policy, the beneficial consequences of free flows of goods, finance capital, ideas, and persons between societies, and the favorite idea that international conflicts should be settled through legal machinery. Most of the work in general international politics, however, was hyper-factual and overly prone to preaching.

In the two decades following World War I, serious debates about the appropriate forms of a discipline took place, and there was a growing awareness that the purpose of the study should be to develop generalizations about patterns of behavior and recurring phenomena, to emphasize that which was common to most nations, rather than unique events. By the 1940s, in short, English and American scholars had come to a position developed several centuries previously. As seen in the works of E. H. Carr, Martin Wight, Hans Morgenthau, and others, the new era of theoretical effort demonstrated clearly that the classical problematic of Grotius, Saint-Pierre, Hobbes, Rousseau, and Kant still provided the framework around which analysis in the field should be organized.

The Causes of War and the Conditions of Peace/Security/Order

In Thucydides' account of the Peloponnesian Wars, the reader does not discern in the author a feeling of moral condemnation of the slaughter and destruction of the battles. To be sure, there were damaging effects on the internal life of the *poleis*, and the wars often featured a mix of stupidity, poor leadership, bad luck, and tactical errors. But killing, looting, and casting prisoners into slavery seemed to be the natural consequences of a ubiquitous phenomenon of political life, war. Thucydides disapproved of the killing of prisoners, but otherwise was not sufficiently outraged by the inhumanity of the wars to suggest any proposals for remedying the incessant military clashes between the city states.

Almost two thousand years later, in contrast, Grotius, a witness to the wholesale destruction of the Thirty Years' War, and Hobbes, who was willing to establish an all-powerful Leviathan to overcome the turmoil typical of the English Civil War, were greatly concerned about organized violence. While by today's standards the wars of the seventeenth and eighteenth centuries were not notably destructive, they had become a sufficiently unpleasant feature of the European landscape to compel a number of writers to seek ways to prevent them, or to reduce their costly consequences should they occur. For Rousseau and Kant, moreover, the militarization of royal regimes, the wars fought to generate a firmer grip on their subjects' loyalty—the old stratagem of creating an external enemy to consolidate domestic support—and the conspicuous waste of scarce resources on military campaigns rendered domestic political reform more difficult.[1] War, then, was the acknowledged problem, to be both explained and overcome.

In the most famous works of these centuries, the diagnoses of war causation were not particularly well developed, at least by today's standards. With the exception of Rousseau, the other commentators devoted much more thought to the consequences of the problem and the means of overcoming it than to its etiology. For Grotius, Hobbes, and Kant, for example, the causes were located in human nature: greed, pride, and covetousness. Little else was said about the matter. Hobbes's radical individualism, his view of man in the state of nature, was sufficient to account for man as a leader of a state. Although the behavior of states in a states system is not perfectly parallel to man in the state of nature (see below), the reasons for the differences lie not in conceptions of human nature, in the natural state compared to political roles, but rather in the muting effects of mutual deterrence, necessary prudence, and rudimentary international norms.

Rousseau's analysis of war is more complex—and more sophisticated—because he located its origins at the individual, social, and systemic levels. In Rousseau's state of nature, man is essentially peaceful and sociable. As Clark points out, "it is the move from the state of nature to civil society that makes man a fighter" (1980, 62). There is nothing inherent in human nature, as Hobbes would have it, that predisposes man to aggression. Society corrupts man by instilling in him the development of artificial needs, as personified in the activities of kings and princes.[2] War, then, is pre-eminently a *social* undertaking; it does not exist until there are citizens; soldiers are made from citizens, not from "natural" man.

In his critique of the Abbé Saint-Pierre's scheme for a European federation, however, Rousseau emphasized the role of individual passion both as a cause of conflict and as a sufficient reason why overall peace plans will not work. He made a general observation about human nature in civil society, outlined in a letter to Mirabeau: "My friends! you must allow me to tell you that you give too much weight to your calculations, and too little to the heart of man and the play of passion.... [Saint-Pierre's] system is excellent for Utopia; for the children of Adam it is worth nothing" (Rousseau n.d., 16). But in his strong denunciation of despotism and the suggestion, written elsewhere, that a system of states composed of autonomous republics might be a sufficient condition for peace, he also proposed that the causation of war lies not in the individual qua citizen, but in the *kinds of regimes*, a hypothesis that has commanded significant research energies in recent years.

But even here we are not certain of Rousseau's ultimate views on the subject of war causation because in other parts of his analyses of international matters he predicted reasonable stability between relatively autonomous republics, indicating that it is the connection between units, as much as the nature of the units, that causes conflict. His analysis of the detrimental effects of interdependence further substantiates this view. The level of explanation thus shifts from the individual and societal regime, to the systemic, suggesting that citizens, regimes, and states are necessary but not sufficient causes of war. But connection is not sufficient either; it is the consequences of plural or many connections that are the crux of the matter.

Rousseau's parable of the stag hunt is perhaps the most succinct and well-known statement of the systemic sources of international conflict and war. Yet it is not a statement of necessity, only of possibility or probability. The "security dilemma" is inherent in a system of independent but connected states. Though states might, like a group of hunters organized to track a single stag, collaborate in order to maximize everyone's gain, there is always the possibility of defection, suggested by the hunter who makes a grab for a *sure* meal, a rabbit, and thereby ruins the opportunity of killing the stag. The ever-present possibility of defection creates permanent distrust among the units of the system, leads to calculations of short-term gain ("apparent interest") rather than following the "real" interest of states, which is the common good, and renders regulative devices such as international law largely ineffective.[3]

Rousseau's insights and hypotheses have formed the basis of innumerable studies of general international politics, providing the foundation of what is often called the "realist" tradition. Rousseau's voice is heard in virtually every analysis which emphasizes the ubiquitousness of power politics, and in the laments of those frustrated by governments' consistent inability to escape from harmful and resource-wasting arms races. And the dozens of peace plans that have been elaborated in the last two hundred years, but which did not pay attention to Rousseau's analyses, have all foundered for reasons clearly specified by him.

Most theorists of the seventeenth and eighteenth centuries offered no analysis of war causation of similar persuasiveness. They were more interested in illuminating the paths to peace than in diagnosing the malady. If the source of war is located in human nature, in any case, there is little that can be done at that level. With the exception of Kant, none of the theorists argued that man can learn, or can be educated away from the personality defects that lead to war (this idea develops in the nineteenth century and is still common today). Hence, solutions must be found at the levels of individual states or in the states system. Here, there are three distinct approaches: (1) develop and enhance constraints already existing within the system; (2) create new international institutions to regulate aggressors; and (3) plans which require the transcendence of the system.

For Grotius, the solution lies in laws which to a large measure already exist. The purpose is not to eliminate wars but rather to offer criteria which, as in the medieval tradition, would distinguish legitimate or just wars from illegitimate armed undertakings. Only those wars which are waged for self-defense, enforcement of rights, or on behalf of community goals (for example, the perpetuation of the system of states) are legitimate, whereas those waged for purely selfish (national) aggrandizement are not (Parkinson 1977, 36). As Hedley Bull points out (1966, 52) this criterion of legitimacy indicates an assumption of a genuine international society, a community interest.

Underlying the community is a legal system, the *ius gentium*, or law of nations, which provides significant restraints against self-centered action. The law of nations is based on practice and usage (custom) and on the testimony of learned scholars. While it reflects community norms, its ultimate sanction is self-interest. "Just as the national, who violates the law of his country in order to obtain an immediate advantage, breaks down that by which the advantage of himself and his posterity are for all future time assured, so that state which transgresses the law of nature and of nations cuts away also the bulwarks which safeguard its own future peace" (quoted in Russell 1936, from Grotius 1925, II:18). In other words, unlike Rousseau's pessimistic conclusion that princes could never pursue the common interest because of the possibility of defection, Grotius suggests that governments typically calculate self-interests in terms of a reckoning of long-range interests, which are synonymous with the community interest. International law serves as an effective restraint because its precepts join the ultimate interests of the individual state—independence—with the interests of the community. Independence and the common good are not incompatible; hence, peace can be secured through continued development of the law of nations, buttressed also by the law of nature.

Hobbes, who is often miscast as the father of a particularly pessimistic form of realism, a war of all against all, acknowledged several means of muting international conflict. For example, he conceded the possibility of a convergence of interests between states (Hoffmann 1965, 67) and observed that in wars and conflict between states, unlike civil wars, "a certain mean was wont to be observed" (Parkinson 1977, 39). Deterrence creates prudence. He also accorded natural law a restraining influence. But Hobbes proposed no "plan" for perpetual peace and thus, like Grotius, he is a minimalist in terms of proposed solutions to the problem. Indeed, since Hobbes makes no suggestion that wars can be permanently eliminated, he took a significantly less sanguine view toward international war compared to civil war (Hoffmann 1965, 61). Possibly it is for this reason that the solution to violence in the state of nature—the contract establishing the Leviathan—is not proposed as a solution for interstate war.

Saint-Pierre and Rousseau, to list only the best-known, had more grandiose objectives. Though with quite different results, they outlined proposals for new sets of international institutions to take care of the problem of war once and for all. They were both maximalists. The Abbé Saint-Pierre, in *A Project for Making Peace Perpetual in Europe* (1927), outlined a scheme for organizing the Christian states of Europe into a federal union. This voluminous text of more than 1,200 pages was based on the Abbé's distress with the suffering caused by the War of the Spanish Succession (1702–13) and his concern about the war's escalation throughout the continent. According to the scheme, the Christian princes were to renounce the use of force except to carry out the judgments of the whole organization. They would be obliged as well to submit all conflicts to a general assembly. The organization was also to have bureaux concerned with commercial and legal matters, foreshadowing the specialized agencies of the League of Nations and United Nations more than two hundred years later. The plan stirred much interest, but also elicited numerous critiques for its lack of realism (Russell 1936, 188–91).

Among them was Rousseau's own blueprint for peace. His proposal, which he himself rejected as impracticable given the shortsightedness of princes and kings, is also the creation of a confederation of states, but with limited enforcement powers (Clark 1980, 62–3). It would be akin to a social contract between states. According to Hoffmann, however (1965, 80), Rousseau really envisaged a defensive league of small states, none of which would sacrifice sovereignty; it thus resembled the idea of a defensive alliance rather than Saint-Pierre's system of a collective peacekeeper.

But perhaps Rousseau's preferred solution to the problem of war is a world constituted of small republics, each sufficiently autonomous and self-sufficient to keep at a minimum a need for international contacts. The view that transactions between states would lead to peace and stability finds a firm refutation in Rousseau's writings. Given the increasing size, population, and military differentiation of states in eighteenth-century Europe, as well as growing commercial interdependence, Rousseau's solution appears no less utopian than Saint-Pierre's; indeed, it is not a maximalist plan in the sense of creating new institutions from the existing system, but comes closer to the third type of peace proposal, which requires transcendence of the system.

But it was Kant who is the true spokesman of the third avenue to peace. The ultimate goal is a global community of individuals, even if along the way a confederation of republics, à la Rousseau, would be necessary. Unlike Saint-Pierre, who had an eye (even if a naive one) to the political acceptability of his scheme in Europe's royal courts, Kant held that only republics (meaning constitutional orders) could become members of his initial confederation of states. This requirement was based on his view that wars are basically the folly of princes. When the people have power, they will be reluctant to engage in war because it is they, ultimately, who "pay the cost of war out of their own pockets, miserably repair the devastation that it leaves behind, and to add to the over-abundance of misery, they themselves have to bear the burden of debts which, owing to ever new wars, could never be paid off and would thus embitter peace itself" (Kant 1957, 13).

The objective of such a confederation is the free flow of people, goods, and ideas, a world in which "the individual's rights come to transcend the boundaries of his own nation, being secured . . . not by any supranational authority, but by the mutual recognition, among the confederate states, of their rights and duties *vis-à-vis* each other's nationals" (Gallie 1978, 27). This seems far removed from the problem of war, but like many nineteenth-century English liberals (and earlier French *philosophes*), Kant assumed that these sorts of individual-to-individual contacts would produce pacific relations between states that respect the rule of law at home and abroad. Ultimately, a genuine world society, or cosmopolis, would emerge through various routes. The states on the road to that future system would become more homogeneous in terms of constitution, ideology, and religion, thus enhancing solidarity; otherwise, a "single country will be the standard bearer of legitimacy" and will unify the world (Wight 1966a, 94). All of this would be made possible because men would increasingly learn the bitter lessons from ever-intensifying wars between nation states (Gallie 1978, 32). They would *learn* the necessity of collaborating to produce the common good.

Units of Analysis and Essential Actors

In most of these statements of the problem and proposed

22

remedies, the discussion is set in terms of the actions of states within the context of a European states system. Only sovereignties are members of that system. Grotius, reflecting the continued existence of late medieval nonstate actors into the seventeenth century, pays some attention to "private wars," but the brunt of his analysis is the relationship between the *ius gentium* and the activities of states.

Rousseau and Kant, both admirers of republicanism and vigorous critics of royal despotism, blamed specific wars (if not the phenomenon of war itself) on the proclivities of royalty. Unrestrained by popular moods or society-wide needs, they recklessly sought foreign dominions and, in Kant's view, regarded war as a sport or pleasure party to be initiated for "trivial reasons" (Kant 1957, 13). There was thus the hint from Kant and the more explicit analysis of Rousseau—in his discussion of real versus apparent interests—that the interests of states are not necessarily synonymous with the interests of royal leadership. This tendency to disaggregate the state, to locate war causation in types of regimes, is less well developed than is, for example, Rousseau's analysis of the consequences of a system of states.

But even if some royal regimes did not "represent" true state interests, there was no question that the field of inquiry involved only the actions and interactions of *states*, no matter who their spokesmen. Eighteenth-century thinkers acknowedged neither the existence nor importance of nonstate actors, as those are defined today. States and the system of states—the essential actors and their behavior, the units of analysis—remained the centerpieces of the study of international politics from the seventeenth century until the 1970s.

Images of the World

The nature of world images is obviously linked with the first two criteria that define paradigms in international theory. But we can separate it for purposes of analyzing one major debate among our seventeenth- and eighteenth-century thinkers, the degree of order and society among the states in the system. We should recall, first, that all the writers in question were speaking of the European states system, and not of a global system such as exists today. They had little to say about the treatment of "savages" beyond the continent, although this had been a matter of considerable debate among international lawyers such as

Vitoria. Nor did they seem particularly concerned about the role of the Muslim infidel in the states system. Their concern was war and order among the kingdoms and principalities of continental Europe. The characteristics which made this a single system will be discussed in more detail in the next chapter, but they can be summarized here.

Europe was more than a mere geographical expression; although it was politically carved up into separate states there were sufficient bonds uniting them that it was not stretching reality to talk of a "society of states." Princes and subjects were alike members of "Christendom," joined by many of the attributes of a common religion, culture, and types of political order. The elites were cosmopolitan Europeans, sharing tastes in music, theatre, architecture, literature, and art. Their members regularly served in foreign courts as royal advisers and military leaders. And there were no major ideological cleavages which established permanent enmities between the royal houses, although the conflict between the Habsburgs and Bourbons was more than a passing matter. In short, the units of the system shared much in common. Perhaps it was this characteristic that so concerned our writers: given the commonalities, the attributes the states shared, and the fact of a common civilization, the European states *should* have been less war-prone.

The notion of independent states operating within some sort of order is common to the creators of the classical tradition (Rousseau is a possible exception), but the degree of order, or the existence or nonexistence of a "society" of states was and continues to be a matter of debate. For Grotius, the analogy of law in domestic society is applied to the international realm (Wight 1966b, 38–9), with the result that differences between them are of degree, not of kind. Grotius explicitly developed the idea of an international society (Bull 1966, 52), a moral entity entitling some actors to engage in war to preserve it for the good of all (Savigear 1978, 40). The diplomatic world, then, is not just a domain of autonomous states sharing only propinquity, where war and its threat are the norms of intercourse. To Grotius, they are a deviation, a reflection of the incompleteness and inadequacies of the norms which do in fact provide a good deal of order in this international society.

Hobbes, often portrayed as a Machiavellian admitting of no restraints except those of deterrence, in fact acknowledged a number of conflict-reducing mechanisms whose operations imply some form of international order. These include the laws of nature, prudence (the recognition that constant warfare would derogate from the subjects' loyalties), and the possibility that a more highly developed international law might lead to a "troubled peace" rather than to recurring war (Hoffmann 1965, 61). We should recall, too, that Hobbes spoke of a "posture of war" as the permanent and typical characteristic of international politics—not a bad description of Soviet-American relations during the last four decades—and not of constant violence. His metaphor is the gladiator *poised* for combat, not the actual melée.[4] Thus, while Hobbes would not concede the existence of a society of states in the sense of a group of actors typically sharing common objectives and effectively restrained by rules of the game, at least the consequences of prudence, rudimentary international law, and the idea of reciprocity result in some type of stability. He differed from Grotius primarily because the locus of order was located in the units themselves, and was not a characteristic of a system.

Rousseau was even more pessimistic in his characterization of the world of European states. Those elements of the system which other writers had extolled as instruments of order and stability were to Rousseau exactly the opposite: the means which states use for self-aggrandizement. Many balance of power theorists of the eighteenth century had argued that the diplomacy of equilibrium not only provided for peace, but was also an essential mechanism for maintaining the states system against the hegemonic drives of the Habsburgs and Louis XIV. Grotius, Pufendorf, Suarez, and Vattel had all expounded on the means by which the law of nations served as a means of rendering commerce and other forms of interaction between states safe, stable, and reliable.

To Rousseau, however, balances, agreements, and laws were, like deceit, diplomacy, and war, just instrumentalities for aggrandizement (Hoffmann 1965, 67). The balance of power, while it might indeed preserve the system, nevertheless perpetuated instability. The world, then, is devoid of meaningful restraints and the areas of common agreement are insignificant and short-lasting. His notion of the benefits of autonomy in the state of nature led him to conclude, in opposition to the physiocrats and young advocates of free trade, that commerce—indeed all forms of interstate contact—breed conflict. More than Hobbes, Rousseau represents the opposite to Grotius's viewpoint.

Kant shared Rousseau's pessimism about the capacity of the

states system to operate on any other basis than state expansion, war, domestic despotism, and instability. What exactly Kant had in mind as the ultimate shape of the world remains a matter of some disagreement among the experts.[5] There is agreement, however, in the importance Kant placed on developing links between people, not states, and in the potential of human solidarity. Employing an analytical device somewhat akin to Rousseau's distinction between real and apparent interests, Kant advanced the view that the essential nature of international relations is not conflict between states (the apparent relationship) but is "really the relationship among all men in the community of mankind ... which exists potentially even if it does not exist actually" (Bull 1977, 25). Within this community, the interests of men are the same, whereas in the existing political realm conflicts of interest exist only between the ruling despotic cliques. As suggested, the experience of ever-increasingly destructive wars would ultimately lead to the transformation of the states system and the emergence of something more consistent with the "universal" interest. Peace and order, or society, will come, then, not through the development of mechanistic artifacts, such as the balance of power or Saint-Pierre's peace organization, but rather with "the quest for justice between men through justice between states" (Gallie 1978, 3).[6] Kant has the image of some type of *world* organization that is consistent with the fact of a universal moral community, something more worthy than the world of European states.

Two points need to be raised from this brief review of the use of the three criteria by the classical authors of international theory. First, the models of the world, the notions of the states system or, for Kant, a world community, were *ideal* types, devoted to illuminating the essential characteristics of the units of analysis, the actions of states in the context of a states system. They should be judged, then, not from the point of view of historical accuracy, but from their ability to reveal or predict typical forms of behavior, and the logical outcomes of the system's structure. We would say the same in assessing, for example, Morton Kaplan's (1957) models of international systems.

Second, the nature of the states system—our third criterion—has been a question of such importance that it has been used as a basis sufficient in itself to establish different schools *within* the classical tradition. Though using somewhat different labels,

Otto von Gierke (1955, 235–7),[7] Martin Wight (1966b) and
Hedley Bull (1977) have all summarized the main world images
under the rubrics of the Hobbesian, Grotian, and Kantian traditions. The key question dividing them, as suggested, is the
degree of order, the presence or absence of the quality of a
"society" of states.[8] When the other two criteria—the
war/peace problematic and the units of analysis/essential
actors—are added, we have even stronger evidence of
theoretical work that has established "a coherent tradition,"
that is, a single paradigm.

The Nineteenth Century: Optimism of the Liberals

There were no figures in the century and one-half following
Rousseau and Kant who could compare in comprehensiveness
of analysis about international politics, who elaborated in such
detail on each of the three criteria. There was, however, a body
of thought, starting with Jeremy Bentham's *Plan for Universal
and Perpetual Peace* (1789), which we might call the liberal tradition. It was essentially Grotian, but had unique views on the
role of publics and international commerce, reflecting the
nineteenth-century development of international commerce,
democracy, nationalism, and the era of growing prosperity and
peace. Since our purpose is not to present an intellectual history
of international theory, but to demonstrate the continuing
importance of the three criteria in determining approaches to
the study, we will not investigate each author, but rather
generalize about the body of thought; this of course will lead to
some distortion, by emphasizing similarity and continuity,
while relegating differences (some of which are theoretically
important) to the periphery.

The liberals tended to attribute the causes of war to types of
political regimes—particularly to royal despotisms—rather than
to the system itself. There was a general antipathy to the "continental" ways of conducting international politics, and a corresponding assumption that democratic politics would avoid the
power politics typical of eighteenth-century Europe. Bentham,
for example, attributed war to passions, ambitions, insolence,
and a desire for power, all likely to be located in autocratic
political systems (but not in republics), where the people were
more concerned with grandeur through foreign conquests.
Bentham also saw war as a consequence of feudal remnants

where matters of succession and family patrimony rather than social needs determined diplomatic interests. Like Rousseau and many modern observers, Bentham regarded war as reflecting the insecurity of elites (Hinsley 1967, 83-8; cf. Rosecrance 1963). Later liberals extended the fault to all governments, contrasting the essential community of interests between societies, with an apparent natural disharmony among governments. This view was later revised back to its original form, particularly by Americans who had to locate scapegoats for the origins of World War I. Thus, Woodrow Wilson shared Bentham's dislike of autocracy and added for good measure the elements of the system of the great powers in action, including secret diplomacy, alliances, the balance of power, and militarism. Earlier liberals would have added the vice of mercantilism.

The conditions for peace, security, and order followed logically from these diagnoses of war causation. In place of the insecure elites of the absolutist states, democracy was necessary; and in many of the British versions around mid-nineteenth century, the democracy should include as little government intervention as possible. Since it was assumed that there were no fundamental incompatibilities between the economic interests of various societies, an international regime of the free flow of trade, finance, and people would enhance the ties that bind the "family of nations." Peace, then, was the predicted consequence of free transactions (an idea also developed by the French *philosophers*: see Hinsley 1967, 83) while continued economic prosperity would act as a powerful disincentive to future wars (Parkinson 1977, 93). Public opinion, which had no interest in conflict, should be sufficient to make governments obey the essential rules of international law; there was, then, no need to construct supranational institutions, which would add just another layer of government. The only necessary device would be an international tribunal to resolve the few disputes that might arise between countries. For the most optimistic, institutions were also no longer necessary because peace had become the natural condition among sophisticated, progressive peoples, tied together as they were by the bonds of shared economic interests and, in today's parlance, interdependence.

The unit of action initially remained the state, although some used the term nation with increasing regularity, implying a distinction between the more conflict-prone tendencies of governments, and the inherently peaceful proclivities of citizens. We thus get the possibility of transnational relations, that growing profusion of individual contacts, the nature and interests of which may differ significantly from the interests of governments, and particularly of governments of the old order. The model of international politics with the state as the only actor is now enlarged to provide for theoretical examination of individuals and international nongovernmental organizations.

The image of the world thus gains a new dimension, a kind of normative dichotomization. In its simplest form, it is the distinction between the world of transnational relations, in which interaction is characterized by competition and collaboration, and the world of the diplomat and warrior, where conflict remains the typical activity. The elements of order in the first domain—public opinion, mutual social interests in trade and investment, and the continued codification of international law to regulate the ever-growing transnational activities—will, it is hoped, "spill over" to provide stability in the diplomatic realm. There is less discussion of a society of states, and more emphasis on a community of nations or "family of nations." The vision is Grotian in the sense that a community implies more than a random collection of political entities and in the importance attributed to international law; but in locating a crucial restraining device, public opinion, *within* the state it has a perspective that is more in the Hobbesian mode.

The liberal view of international politics and relations had a pervasive effect on the academic study of the field throughout the first four decades of this century, and continues to inform research in areas such as integration and interdependence. Most analyses of international relations in these decades expressed the optimistic views that the progress of mankind, indicated by the League of Nations, the Hague Court, self-determination, free trade, and the lessons learned from the "war to end all wars," were sufficient to render the parable of the stag hunt obsolete. World War I, particularly among American analysts, had been insufficient to shake the faith of those steeped in the liberal view.

They saw the carnage essentially as the last gasp of the old order, the death throes of the Hobbesian (or more accurately, the Rousseauian) version of international politics; few saw it as just another eruption of the classic state system, a normal and expected event. The liberals predicted—or hoped—it would not happen again, for elite insecurity and the mechanisms used to conduct the diplomacy of the old states system—secret diplomacy, alliances, and balance of power—had been at least partly purged from the Wilsonian postwar order.

The Return to Rousseau

World War II had a very different effect on international relations scholarship. The generation of academics that was to define the field in the 1940s and 1950s saw the war as evidence that the world according to Rousseau really had not changed. The old game of power politics was still with us. Processes, interests, and outcomes were basically unchanging. What was regular in international life was war, conflict, balances, alliances, and spheres of influence, combined with some forms of restraint. Rousseau's pessimism reigned in the analyses of Morgenthau, Carr, Schwartzenberger, and others, although adherents of the liberal tradition struggled vigorously in the debate between "realists" and "idealists" during the 1950s. International organization as a solution to the problem of war and turmoil continued to be popular for another two decades, but in general the theoretical and most of the descriptive studies of the postwar decades were imbued with the concepts, terminology, and overall pessimism of Hobbes and Rousseau. The Grotian view of the world may have provided a reasonable portrait of relationships within the "free world," but given the character of the cold war, wherein both antagonists basically rejected the notion that there could be two types of societies inhabiting a single international order, the terminology of an international society or family of nations seemed at odds with the diplomatic and military realities.

Since the works of the major figures in international theory of the postwar period are well known, it is not necessary to review how each dealt with the three criteria. There were differences, of course, but the areas of agreement are more prominent. The causes of war lie in the struggle for power and the eternal security dilemma which make every state's efforts to provide security for itself the cause of another state's insecurity.[9] The never-ending purpose of the game of international politics is to increase power; there is no possibility of dropping out of the game. The actors are states, although some transnational organizations such as the Comintern and Cominform have to be mentioned, at least as instrumentalities of the power game. Authorities such as Morgenthau denied that international organizations such as the United Nations have an influence of their own. They are institutions of multilateral diplomacy, inherently connected to the interests of the major powers. They are arenas of power politics, not agencies for transformation of the system.

There is continued concentration on the questions of war, peace, security, and order. The nature of power becomes a critical theoretical issue, largely neglected by the liberals. It makes no difference how rich the tableau of transnational relations; Morgenthau, Carr, Schuman, and the others do not analyze these actors or processes simply because they are not interested in phenomena that are demonstrably unconnected to a parsimonious analysis of the classical problematic. International financial flows, the diplomacy of the Olympic Games, or the operations of an American copper company in Chile may be newsworthy, but they shed little light on the activities and processes that lead to war or enhance peace, security, and order.

The return to Rousseau involved a recommitment to the construction of ideal types, to exploration of the logic of a system wherein no single authority represents the community interest. The separation of "popular" and transnational interests from the interests of governments, a feature of nineteenth-century liberal thought, was either recombined or ignored in the works of most postwar scholars. History had shown that public opinion and democracy, combined with the politics of economic welfare, were not sufficient conditions for fundamentally transforming the nature of international politics. Nor did a cataclysmic war, the United Nations, and the pax Americana render concepts such as alliances, balancing, and diplomacy obsolete. The old truths of Hobbes and Rousseau continued to establish the problematic of international theory. And certainly it was not altered by introducing new methodologies in inquiry.

The "Behavioral Revolution" and the Study of International Politics

To this point the essay has sought to demonstrate the continuity of a long tradition of international theory. While there have been important differences between the Rousseau and liberal views of the world, the similarities of approach toward the three criteria —the subject of study, units of analysis/essential actors, and images of the world (except Kant's ultimate cosmopolis)—are notable. The search for essentials, for patterns and recurrence, the normative concern with the war and peace problem, and the debates concerning the existence and/or effectiveness of legal and other types of order-producing mechanisms, have united the figures into a coherent tradition.

Some have claimed that the "behavioral revolution" constituted a watershed, that it effectively challenged the classical tradition and launched a new research agenda. This position has been elaborated most explicitly by Arend Lijphart (1974). Some others, who dismissed the works of the founding fathers as just so many impressionistic and often biased personal statements, did not necessarily claim a paradigmatic shift occasioned by the introduction of quantitative techniques, but they implied that there was not much worthy of emulation or development in the classical paradigm anyway; the "behavioral revolution" represented a new wave, one that would produce knowledge qualitatively different from its predecessors.

Lijphart makes the most elaborate case that the new wave in fact represented a paradigmatic shift, and was not merely the grafting of more systematic research techniques on to the old questions. Though there were significant differences among the classical writers, he argues (as I do) that they were "clearly guided by a paradigm in the sense of a model or a vision from which springs a 'coherent tradition ... of scientific research'" (1974, 49, quoting Kuhn). He places Grotius, however, into a different tradition because the Dutch writer regarded the international normative consensus "as sufficiently strong and pervasive to render the image of the state of nature, even in the Lockean sense, inapplicable" (p. 50). He thus uses the degree of order and the existence of normative restraining elements in the system as the criterion for distinguishing paradigms.

Lijphart contends that the "behavioral revolution" produced a new paradigm because it included a "distinctive substantive metaphor ... systems theory" (p. 63). The classical tradition, in his view, worked with a model of anarchy, characterized by a fundamental distinction between the nature of domestic and international politics. In contrast, most behavioralists are indifferent to the distinction, or in fact adopt a metaphor of an international system "that is analogous to the domestic political system—a metaphor which bears a striking resemblance to the Grotian conception of a world society" (p. 64).

Even though Lijphart acknowledges that balance of power and collective security ideas are also forms of systems theory, he argues vigorously that the Grotian world image is sufficiently different from the views held by Hobbes, Locke, and Rousseau as to constitute an entirely separate paradigm. Hence, the "gap dividing the contending approaches [of Hobbes versus Grotius] is as wide as the one between Snow's 'two cultures.' In fact, the cleavage between these two cultures ... coincides with the difference between the traditional and behavioural approaches" (p. 62). The first modern comprehensive study employing the Grotian systems metaphor, according to Lijphart, is the Deutsch et al. investigation of integration into amalgamated and pluralistic security communities. The revolutionary idea in this work is the possibility of permanent peace, in the pluralistic security community, between independent states; that is, lasting peace in a context of international anarchy (p. 64). This conclusion flies in the face of the consequences of the "state of war" posited by Hobbes and Rousseau.

Lijphart might have added that Deutsch's work also differed from the classical tradition in failing to use state activity as the essential unit of analysis in the independent variables. His notion of transactions between nonstate actors, foreseen by the nineteenth-century liberals, offers a significant deviation from the analytical habits of the classical paradigm. The addition of Deutsch's nonstate actors may not, however, signify a paradigm shift because the end product of integration into pluralistic security communities is the peaceful relationship between *states*—the classical problematic—not just peoples. The outcome of interaction in Deutsch's work is fundamentally at odds with Rousseau's predictions (but remember that Rousseau was discussing ideal types, which did not preclude "islands of peace" in the system), but the theme of peace and war guides Deutsch's work, just as it did his predecessors'.

This is not the place to quarrel with Lijphart's interpretation of the Grotian world image, or with the view that the systems metaphor is fundamentally different from the "state of war" metaphor. But differences in a *single* feature of the states system are not sufficient in my opinion to signify the existence of different paradigms, so long as the units of analysis, actors, and the problematic remain essentially the same. I would argue that there has to be a shift in at least two of the criteria, and preferably all three, to constitute a fundamental change in the field. Grotius keeps the Hobbes problematic and essential actors. Deutsch, as is the case with most of the work in integration theory, also keeps the problematic, the essential actors (though disaggregated in the independent variables into social transaction flows), and the metaphor of international anarchy, that is, the absence of a universal authority. The object of integration is not to transcend the system, à la Kant, but to aggregate once-separate (and quarreling) states into larger collectivities having all the attributes of a state.

A brief review of some of the main areas of inquiry, those employing quantitative techniques and/or behavioral concepts will help support the case that there is a fundamental continuity between the classical tradition and the products of the behavioral revolution. In the first place, the problematic has not changed. The normative concern with the causes of war and the conditions of peace/security/order has continued to guide research and teaching. For example, the notion of decision-making has spawned a large literature on the problem of misperception, particularly in crisis situations. There is a clear assumption underlying this literature that misperception is a major problem that can lead to war. Some of the writing is explicitly normative in outlining administrative and technical means that could reduce the possibilities of such phenomena as "group-think," decisions made on the basis of inadequate or faulty information, or choices conditioned excessively by personal (political or psychological) needs.[10] The already vast but still growing literature on international crises using states and their interactions as units of analysis, also demonstrates a normative concern with war-avoidance. The purpose is not merely to uncover patterns of behavior, but, should those exist, to identify those types of crises or behaviors that are most likely to lead to war. In this research, some of the conditions necessary for peace and security are implied to be the reverse of the causes of crises and war. Without misperceptions, without "group-think," without overly rigid commitments in deterrence situations; or *with* multiple option advocacy and with clear communication between crisis adversaries, perhaps war can be avoided. These and many others appear to be "lessons" learned from recent research, lessons which are centrally related to the classical problematic.

A debate that goes back at least to the seventeenth century continues today among researchers. Is peace best preserved by an approximate balance of power between major contenders, or by a predominance of power by the status-quo oriented state or groups of states? An extensive body of work has sought to link various configurations of power to the incidence of war and to the preservation of peace. While the findings have been contradictory or inconclusive, apparently a significant number of scholars in the last two decades have thought the questions raised by the classical analysts to be sufficiently important, in terms of shedding light on the traditional core concerns of the field, to warrant a considerable expenditure of funds and time. A subset of this question, the relationships between alliances and war, has occupied almost two decades of a major research project at the University of Michigan.

Rousseau, Kant, many nineteenth-century liberals, as well as Marxists, have argued that certain types of regimes are more war-prone than others. This idea has also been subjected to extensive research, with the conclusion that there is no *significant* relationship between the two variables—although in his newest work Rummel (1983) uncovers an inverse relationship between "libertarian" regimes and war participation. Size, level of economic development, and other variables have also been linked to various forms of external conflict behavior. These were problems not unfamiliar to Montesquieu.

Many studies in international integration or interdependence follow in the tradition of the nineteenth-century liberals, who did not share Rousseau's pessimism and the conclusion that transactions between states and societies were typically conflict-producing. On the contrary, the assumption is that social transactions, in particular, are essentially harmonious and will likely lead to better interstate relations, if not to an integrated community. Most integration studies employing various types of transaction flows as independent variables have similarly assumed that the greater the scope and intensity of such flows, the more likely "integration" would result. Only a few recent essays on "interdependence" have taken the Rousseau position that closer ties between countries and societies, particularly in the areas of trade and resources, may heighten senses of vulnerability and ultimately lead to conflict (Keohane and Nye 1977).[11] Regardless of the particular approach, the animating drive of all inquiry into international integration has been to discover ways and means of overcoming the state of war. The impetus for the uniting of Europe, for example, was not only to increase economic rationalization, expand markets, and eliminate the distorting effects of trade and investment barriers, but primarily to terminate the Franco-German rivalry that had led to one major regional war and two catastrophic world wars in less than seventy years. Monnet's idea of a coal and steel

35

community was a path to peace, not just a mechanism for economic growth.

More directly policy-relevant areas of research have also been formulated within the context of the classical problematic. These include strategic studies, the focus of which has shifted from exploring ways to fight wars, as in the nineteenth-century predecessors, to ways to prevent or deter them. Although there has been a recent revival of war-fighting studies—even with nuclear weapons—the main body of the theoretical literature has been devoted to finding ways of preventing war through manipulating targeting doctrines, developing invulnerable retaliatory capabilities, altering deployment, and instituting unilateral or bilateral arms control measures. The conventional wisdom remains that war prevention can be assured only through organizing armed force. The underlying logic of this position was spelled out in Rousseau's analysis of the states system. With only a few exceptions, such as Costa Rica, all states have armed themselves and few have admitted that it was for any purpose other than peace. The *para bellum* doctrine has not yet been replaced by an effective counter-doctrine, though many have tried to develop one. This is not the result of individual malevolence or the mendacity of bureaucratic-military complexes. Despite personalities, types of regime, or nature of an economy, the security dilemma remains as omnipresent as it was two hundred years ago. No one wastes his or her time reading Rousseau to obtain a fundamental understanding of the modern military situation.

Writings about universal collective security, ways of improving international judicial institutions, peacekeeping, or other means of controlling violence continue to appear but they do not loom so important in the field as they once did. The experiences of World War II and the cold war have rendered many of the assumptions of nineteenth-century liberalism suspect. None of the institutional proposals has directly addressed the causes of war isolated by Rousseau and others. In particular, the problem of trust and distrust, the ever-present possibility of major power defection even in nonwar-related international enterprises (the United States and the Law of the Sea convention), and the continuing influence of "apparent" interests as the loadstar of diplomatic activity have not been effectively treated by those who would create or strengthen international institutions as the most effective route to peace. Indeed, the very notion that peace as a final, or end, state can be "achieved" has become suspect under the influence of a Rousseau-type pessimism.

The most recent international relations research agenda, which seeks to identify the relationship between economic cycles, leadership in the diplomatic system, and the incidence of war, blends all the components of the classical tradition: states as the essential actors, the normative concern with locating the sources of war and the conditions of peace, and an image of a community of states in which there is perpetual movement upwards and downwards in cycles of leadership, rise, and decline. The focus on economic explanations of cyclical patterns, combined with much quantitative research, does not render this work either new or indicative of a paradigm shift. It carries forth the work of several centuries, albeit with new emphases and insights.[12]

This is not an exhaustive list of the various areas of study and research during the past several decades, but it is sufficiently comprehensive to illustrate the continuity between the classical tradition and modern research. Until the recent challenge from dependency theory and the global society paradigms, the problematic of war, peace, and order has commanded the discipline. What of the essential actors/units of analysis?

Here there has been considerable meddling in the sense that many approaches have disaggregated the state into its constituent decision-makers, bureaucracies, and the various roles that public groups can play in initiating or controlling state policies. But there is no evidence in the roster of recent research that decisive (war- and peace-producing) actions are taken by any actors other than states or their agents. No matter at what level of analysis the research is organized, the studies are of crises between states; of perception and cognitive problems among those who commit the state to war or peace; of the integration of states; and of the state organization of military capabilities.

Hobbes, Rousseau, and Kant did not discuss decision-makers or bureaucracies probably because they understood that the critical variances in international politics are not explained at those levels of analysis, but are more or less determined by the nature of the system itself—a position forcefully reiterated by Kenneth Waltz more recently (1979). Today, we commonly assume that significant variation can be explained at the state rather than the system level, perhaps because in comparison to the Europe of the eighteenth century, differences between states in terms of size, type of government, level of development, or other attributes are much greater today. But research organized at the level of states, or of individuals acting as agents of the state, does not change a paradigm; it merely disaggregates the essential actors and focuses on more circumscribed phenomena. It investigates the individual trees that comprise the international politics forest. It is not, however, investigating deer or birds, also denizens of the forest, but actors which are basically irrelevant to whatever might be a horticultural analogy to peace and war—forest fires, for example. Nonstate actors, or units of analysis composed of their activities, in short, have not figured in most of the work that is roughly categorized as "behavioral," some studies of integration being one exception. Academic international politics remains exactly what its name implies: the study of the official relations between states, taken within the context of a system or society of states.

Images of the world, finally, have not changed significantly either. The debates between the pessimistic progeny of Rousseau or Hobbes on the one hand, and the more optimistic Grotians on the other continue in one guise or another. The "systems" of the literature on international systems are most frequently defined in terms of concepts such as power structure, absence or presence of regulative devices, balances or imbalances of power, and typical processes such as diplomacy, commerce, and war. Even when conceptualized in terms of roles, as in Kaplan's work, they are mostly filled by states. In none of the well-known systems metaphors is the conception of the world fundamentally different from those outlined in the classical tradition.

Even in the integration literature, as noted, the idea is not to eliminate states as the essential form of political organization, that is, to transcend the states system; it is, rather, to create a smaller number of states; a world of, say, a dozen regional states compared to one of 158 present units would vastly reduce the probabilities of war because of the reduced number of dyads (Holsti 1980a). In fact, were such a world to come about, it would have distinct parallels with eighteenth-century Europe in terms of the number of key actors.

In other areas of research, the image of the world is largely a quantitative expansion of the European system, admitting, however, that the network of contacts has deepened and broadened considerably. This has not been of sufficiently great consequence to overcome the problem of war or to render the search for peace any less compelling. It is a peace of states, the stability of a system, and the development of order between states that is at question. The behavioral revolution has not altered the theoretical, metaphorical, or normative menu of international politics and theory developed several centuries ago. It *has* fundamentally rearranged the methods used to obtain knowledge. New methodologies do not by themselves create new paradigms. The challenge to the classical tradition comes, then, not from scientific activity, but from scholars and practitioners whose *normative* priorities differ fundamentally from those inhabiting the classical tradition.

Notes: Chapter 2

1   According to Rousseau, "war and conquest without, the encroachments of despotism within give each other mutual support" (Rousseau n.d., 96–7).

2   The most elaborate analyses of Rousseau's thoughts on war and peace, in the English international relations literature, are Hoffmann 1965, ch. 3, and Waltz 1959, ch. 6. There are some areas of disagreement between the two analyses.

3   "Apparent interest" is "found in the state of absolute independence which frees sovereigns from the reign of law only to put them under that of chance" (Rousseau n.d., 95).

4   Current detractors of the "realist" paradigm criticize it, among other reasons, for its excessive pessimism in viewing international politics as a struggle for power. Many commentators see Hobbes as the originator of this version of diplomatic life; they often criticize the "Hobbesian" world on the grounds that obviously not all international politics is a "war of all against all". Hobbes did not portray international relations in this way; this was a reference to *man* in the state of nature, not to states in the European system. Hobbes summarizes his view on "the state of war" as follows: "For 'war' consists not in battle only or in the act of fighting, but in a tract of time wherein the will to contend by battle is sufficiently known, and therefore the notion of 'time' is to be considered in the nature of war, as it is in the nature of weather. For as the nature of foul weather does not lie in a shower or two of rain [analogy to war], but in an inclination thereto of many days together, so the nature of war does not consist in actual fighting, but in the known disposition thereto during the time there is no *assurance* to the contrary. All other time is 'peace'"(Hobbes 1651, pt. I, ch. 13; my modernization and italics).

5   Interpretations of Kant's views by modern students of international theory vary considerably. cf. Gallie 1978, ch. 1; Bull 1977, esp. pp. 25–6; Hinsley 1967, ch. 4; Clark 1980, ch. 2.

6   Kant's own words are that the federation will "thus establish a continuously growing state consisting of various nations (*civitas gentium*) which will ultimately include all nations of the world" (Kant 1957, 19).

7   I am grateful to Ursula Vollerthun for bringing this work to my attention. She discusses it in her Ph.D. thesis, "The idea of international society" (Vollerthun n.d.).

8   Bull, the primary spokesman for the Grotian tradition in contemporary international theory, suggests that a society of states exists "when a group of states, conscious of certain common institutions and common values, form a society in the sense that they conceive themselves to be bound by a common set of rules in their relations with one another, and share in the working

of common institutions [including] that they should respect one another's claims to independence, that they should honour agreements into which they enter, and that they should be subject to certain limitations in exercising force against one another. At the same time they cooperate in the working of common institutions such as the forms of procedure of international law, the machinery of diplomacy and general international organization, and the customs and conventions of war" (Bull 1977, 13). It might be difficult to operationalize all these characteristics and also to decide "how much" should be present before a society of states exists. In some ways Nazi Germany was a member, but in most others it failed to meet even minimum entrance requirements.

9 There were some analysts who attributed the cause of all problems to the communists; the cause of war does not lie within the system, but can be attributed to certain kinds of states. This is a Wilsonian (but similar in form to Marxist) analysis applied by opponents of the Soviet Union. I do not include these persons in the analysis because they are concerned less with developing international theory than with analyzing the cold war.

10 Readers familiar with recent (for example, last thirty years') literature in international relations research will know the works being referred to in the succeeding paragraphs. The purpose is not to present a literature survey but to demonstrate the continuing influence of the classical tradition in contemporary research. For this reason a comprehensive set of citations is omitted.

11 For case studies of countries enmeshed in asymmetrical "interdependence" situations, see Holsti 1982. Some of Deutsch's work also acknowledges that "too much traffic may cause accidents."

12 The emerging literature on the economic foundations of war is the newest incarnation of the classical tradition, and serves as an important antidote to the field of international political economy which appears to have no normative core. For impressive examples of this genre, see Gilpin 1981; Doran 1983; Väyrynen 1983.

3

A City Common to All:
Theories of Global Society

> Human society is a body of all whose members have a
> common sympathy, so that it is impossible that the
> sickness of one should not be communicated to the
> others. (Crucé 1972, 4)

The "state of war" which was common to the characterization
of international politics by Thucydides, Hobbes, Rousseau, and
many modern theorists was the logical fruit of a world carved
up into separate political communities, each contributing to and
suffering from the security dilemma, and none subject to a central authority. But there is a long tradition of thinking which
starts from a fundamentally different conception of the world—
the global society of individuals, joined together by possessing
in common the faculty of reason, similar capacities for pleasure
and pain, and adhering to common notions of justice. To the
theorists of a global society, war is the product of fragmented
political organization, and not of human nature or type of
regime. The solution to the problem is to transcend or dismantle
the states system and replace it with some sort of order which
is consistent with human solidarity, with common needs and
aspirations. Of the important classical thinkers, only Kant
articulated a cosmopolitan, global order as the ultimate solution
to the problem of war.

His thoughts on the matter had a long ancestry. To appreciate
the continuities and new elements in this tradition, we should
say a few words about its historical origins and its theoretical
antecedents. Otherwise we might accord the newer formulations a degree of novelty not entirely warranted.

41

The Stoic philosophers were not as impressed with the system of independent *poleis* of Greece as Plato and Aristotle had been. City states, according to the Stoics, accentuated divisions among mankind, rather than unity. Their economies were based on the institution of slavery, and the identification of each unit with local deities led to "nationalisms," pride, and prejudice, the outcome of which was often war. Nor could they accept Plato's idea that by reason of superior intellect, some are better equipped to rule, while the remainder should only obey. A world of vertical and horizontal cleavages, representing distinctions of race, class, language, intellect, and caste (slavery), inevitably is a world of political turmoil, rebellion, tyranny, and war. Zeno's comment, "I am a citizen of the world," summarizes a body of thought which emphasized the underlying unity of mankind, the brotherhood of all peoples, and a cosmos as a single whole pervaded by reason, by common notions of justice, and therefore the hope of developing a common system of law.

Despite continual strife, language diversity, and the political fragmentation of medieval Europe, the idea of the unity of Christendom—akin to Stoic, early Christian, and Roman ideals —continued to be significant as a theme of political thought well into the eighteenth century. In Dante's *De monarchia*, a twelfth-century treatise on a universal (meaning Christian) empire, the tradition finds extensive elaboration. The problematic is, among others, war, a virtually ceaseless feature of the medieval landscape. Peace, for Dante, is necessary not just for saving lives, but also to create conditions whereby the individual can develop and realize the full powers of the intellect; Aristotle's notion of the good life can be achieved only when individuals and societies are at peace. The means of achieving it—with Dante perhaps looking more to a past golden age than to a possible future—is universal empire. His notion differed from the Stoic in that it did not call for the abolition of separate kingdoms. But in typical medieval intellectual style, where one worked from the whole to the parts, the idea of an imperial authority representing the common universal interest was the starting point. The kingdoms, although each with its own customs, laws, and interests, existed for the whole. Hence the universal order would have a general law applicable to all parts, regulating their common life, while each of the parts would have self-determined laws regulating matters particular to it (Russell 1936, 101). In this scheme, the analytical units are political bodies, not individuals—hence while the long-range goal may be a global cosmopolis, the reality of separate communities had to be recognized.

Emeric Crucé, whose quote at the beginning of the chapter could serve as a recent statement about human solidarity and interdependence, restores to the tradition of international theory the more perfect form of a universal society composed of individuals, not of kingdoms or any other form representing political fragmentation. "What a pleasure it would be, to see men go here and there freely, to mix together without any hindrance of country, ceremonies, or other such differences, as if the earth were really as it is, a city common to all" (Russell 1936, 165). In this global community, wars would be eliminated because of the priority of the common interest, guaranteed by those characteristics of the human community outlined by the Stoics. Crucé was so imbued by his optimistic vision of human similarity that not even the Christian/infidel dichotomy (so important to Dante) was sufficiently deep to prevent the creation of a single universal political organization devoted to fulfilling man's common needs and purposes. Whatever Cruce's influence, his ideas were notably at odds with the political realities of the day and with the writings of others who were beginning to celebrate the notion of sovereignty.

But the idea of "Christendom," of a family of European princes who share a common destiny as well as common culture, did not die out with the Treaty of Westphalia (1648), any more than it did under the influence of Hobbes's writing. As Hinsley suggests (1967, 107 ff.), it was difficult to distinguish between Louis XIV's major diplomatic objectives, between the interests of the royal house, France, and Christendom. Were they to establish the Bourbon's place in history, to expand France's frontiers through actions of national aggrandizement, or to create a universal monarchy, akin to medieval ideals, throughout the realms of Christendom? The political terminology of the era was replete with references to the Christian community, of which the princes were merely a part. These included terms such as "the Christian Republic," "the Christian world," "the provinces of Christendom," and "the Christian princes of Europe." The Treaty of Utrecht (1713), better known for its specific references to the balance of power, also termed Europe the *Republica Christiana*, implying a community that transcended the collectivity of kingdoms (Hinsley 1967, 171). There was a notion of unity, a moral community with a tradition and sets of rules to maintain. More than one writer believed that it would be possible to reestablish in Europe the structural unity which they thought had existed in medieval times.

The political appeal of the notion of Christendom lay in its ability to generate some unity among the princes in their common struggle against the Turk; but there were other compelling reasons for its popularity as well. Until approximately the middle of the eighteenth century, the description of Europe as a single community was not devoid of cultural, religious, moral, artistic and political content. In 1716 the diplomat François de Callières could write: "Il faut considerer que tous les Etats dont L'Europe est composée, ont entr'eux des liaisons et des commerces necessaires qui font qu'on peut les regarder comme des members d'une même Republique, et qu'il ne peut presque point arriver de changement considerable en quelques uns de ses members qui ne soit capables de troubler le repos de tous les autres" (de Callières 1716, 11). This is a characterization of an interdependent community.

But by the second half of the eighteenth century the elements of order, community, and interdependence seemed to be useless as counterweights to the typical pastime of the princes, which was to wage war against each other, make and unmake alliances, and seek to expand their continental and overseas domains. There are few vestiges of the community ideal remaining in the writings of Rousseau.

It was left to Kant to resurrect the ideal of a community of individuals, to reemphasize the bonds that connect humanity. The primordial confederation of republics does not initially transcend the states system, but as men come to learn the horrendous consequences of ever more destructive wars, their "real" interests will become increasingly visible and they will sweep away the system of states that has brought so much grief and misery. Then there will be an era when the common human interest will prevail, and no matter what the exact political organization of the world, transnational relations will be conducted unhindered by national barriers, and all men will live under a reign of equal rights and duties.

Modern Versions of the Global Society Paradigm

Statements containing important points of similarity with the Stoic, medieval, Crucé, and Kantian tradition appeared intermittently in the nineteenth and early twentieth century, but they became significant as an approach to the study of international politics only after World War II. That war had again underlined the horrendous consequences of the states system's operation. The tradition was perpetuated in the immediate postwar years primarily through the schemes for world peace through world law, which had notable resemblances to some of Dante's ideas (Clark and Sohn 1962). The political units were to remain nation states, but there was to be a universal government, with a monopoly of force, which could act as the guardian of the common interest on questions of peace and war. Unlike the ideas of the Stoics and Kant, however, the various constitutional proposals were not based on a specific view of a global community of individuals tied together by moral bonds and common interpretations of reason and justice.

More recently, new institutes, research programmes, and courses in universities have been devoted to exploring "alternative futures," to developing models of a genuine world or global society, and to studying the techniques necessary for melding the world's great religious and philosophical traditions into a single universal value system. Most of these projects have been associated with the World Order Models Project (WOMP).

Analysts such as John Burton (1972), although not associated with WOMP, have also sought to move beyond the states system paradigm and to visualize the world in terms of a variety of global organizations, networks, and transactions. For some purposes, man is organized into nation states; but for many others—and perhaps for an increasing number of others—they are collected into transnational economic, scientific, cultural, athletic, religious, and many other networks. This conceptualization of the world comes close to another idea developed by authors such as Herbert Spiro (1966) and Richard Mansbach and John Vasquez (1981), who argue that the world should be conceived as a disaggregated set of *issue areas*, where all sorts of actors and agents operate in bargaining and other processes to produce various outcomes. Many of the actors, of course, are individuals and nongovernmental organizations. So the tableau of international politics is not, as the classical tradition would have it, a states system or society of states, but a global system populated by a variety of actors processing issues.

This vision of international politics has certain similarities to the notion of pluralism as a description of the American political system. From our point of view, it is significant because it *assumes* the existence of a genuine political community, where there is reasonable agreement on fundamental procedure, and where outcomes (allocation of values) are for the most part authoritative. One could not develop such an image for a world populated by Attilas and Genghis Khans and perhaps not even for a world of Christian princes. The "processing" of issues by individuals, transnational organizations, and governments sounds very much like the democratic politics of a city, province, or nation—but in this case, in a global community.

This approach has been most explicitly developed at the theoretical level by James Rosenau in his attempts to illuminate a path that will help discard the old states system paradigm (Rosenau 1980). The world in this formulation is comprised of demands and/or actions which are aggregated and disaggregated to produce a variety of outcomes. Thus, "by focussing on aggregations and their spokespersons, we allow ourselves to analyze varied behavior on the global stage without having to presume the importance of states or implicitly making them as more significant than other types of actors. . . . As conceived here, action is located empirically where it originates and is maintained, i.e., in and by individuals. For the only actors in this formulation are the individuals who comprise aggregations and those who serve as spokespersons for them" (p. 151). The virtue of this conceptualization is its emphasis on starting empirically—locating the source of action—and not assuming that actors as abstract as "states" are really the only movers and shakers on the world stage. The metaphor of the stage, while not necessarily suggesting an integrated community, is some sort of organizing device; the units of action are more than a mere collectivity of individuals, totally separate and autonomous. In the process of aggregation, they obviously share interests that either transcend state interests or are different from them. Rosenau is not very explicit about the *sum* of all these actions, but there must be various kinds of linkages between them.

His attempt is perhaps the most explicitly detailed in showing how an alternative to the classical paradigm might be developed for *theoretical* reasons. But neither he nor the others are particularly concerned with causation. Why should there be aggregation in the first place? Is it sufficient to argue that other, non-state types of actors are theoretically and empirically important merely because they exist? Rosenau argues that the actors are significant because there is more interdependence. But is this sufficient reason to create a new paradigm? Rosenau's type of reasoning is not entirely satisfactory because, as some of our quotations have illustrated, the fact of interdependence has long been recognized, but it did not lead to the conclusion that all the actors involved in that interdependence should be the subject of philosophical or empirical inquiry in the field of international politics. The fact of interdependence has to lead to a *problem* before it warrants serious attention, just as concern with war, peace, order, and power led to our field centuries ago.

Andrew Scott provides some of the answers—and raises the right questions which have been missing from many of the global society or issue area models. In his comprehensive analysis of the genesis of international problems (Scott 1982) he provides persuasive reasons why the exclusive focus on state activity may be insufficient for a modern study of international politics. He demonstrates how the ordinary economic activities of the world's population, combined with ever-increasing technological innovation, create such problems as pollution, how the problems and activities combine, and how the world organized in its present fashion cannot develop sufficient managerial capacities to solve or contain them. If the animating condition for power politics is the security dilemma outlined by Rousseau, the force behind the efforts to develop alternative global paradigms is ordinary human activity in a condition of high technology. It is not "interdependence" so much as the universal demand for modern life styles that creates the set of problems.

The approach that most explicitly adopts a stance of modeling a true global society is associated with WOMP. The volume of writing which has emanated from the undertaking is so large and diverse as to defy easy classification; and of course there are many works which are not formally the product of WOMP, but which nevertheless share some of its arguments and outlook.[1] The various approaches share some common characteristics, including notions about fundamental transformations occurring at the global level, a wide range of problems being created by those transformations (not just war), a conviction that nation states are not appropriate agencies for adapting to or managing those problems, a rejection of the nation-state paradigm as offering an adequate analytical platform for either empirical or future-oriented studies, and a fundamental concern for values in addition to peace. The measure is man—development of the human being.

47

The world order studies reject the classical tradition and many of the approaches it has spawned to cope with the problem of war, peace, and order. In its place it proposes new conceptualizations of the world, a vastly extended problematic, and solutions which suggest that the norms of equality and justice are more important than order and stability.

This brief list of major works representing models of global society is by no means exhaustive. Some might argue that it is inappropriate to lump together studies of transnational relations and issue area politics, most of which purport to be descriptive and analytical rather than normative, with world order studies as personified in WOMP, where delineation of ends tends to predominate over rigorous analysis of present realities. Nevertheless, as the following discussion will try to demonstrate, all of the approaches can be considered singly because they share many perspectives on the three criteria that have been designated as central components of international theory paradigms.

The Three Criteria in Global Society Models

The first major shift is in the problematic. While concern with war and peace remains—and in some writings is emphasized because of the consequences of nuclear war—most of the works construct a much broader agenda, one in which the traditional concerns are only one dimension of the problem. In fact, the argument proceeds, given the present and future growth of interdependence, *all* problems have become linked. Global society model proponents, particularly those associated with the WOMP, argue that world peace and security are inseparable from problems such as human rights, ecological balance, income inequality, food distribution and malnutrition, overpopulation, energy scarcity, resource exploitation, and many others. Traditional diplomatic-strategic issues cannot be separated out; they are organically related to global social, cultural, economic, and technological issues. The problematic becomes vastly expanded: it is no less than *the causes of human suffering and the conditions for peace, well-being, social justice, and ecological balance.* Richard Falk sums it up: "My approach to world order ... involves studying the extent to which a given past, present, or future arrangement of power and authority is able to realise a set of human goals that are [*sic*] affirmed as beneficial for all people and apply to

48

the whole world, and achieve some objectivity by their connection with a conception of basic human needs, as required for the healthy development of the human person" (Falk 1977, 180). What is unique about the "problem," aside from its scope, is its source. As Scott has shown, it is not the states system or the "state of war" that generates the new agenda, but the activities of hundreds of millions of humans going about their daily lives in the pursuit of increasing welfare, broadly conceived. The "global crisis" is essentially the crisis of global modernization, the discontinuity between unlimited human wants and the finite capacity of the earth to provide them.

While there is some consensus on the nature of the problems, the methods of overcoming them vary substantially. There is agreement that "old" ways of thinking, structured by the experiences of international politics and nationalism, can only accelerate the trend to doom, and also that effective solutions will have to be both radical and global in perspective. Nation states are not equipped to manage global problems because, in the Rousseauian sense, they are inherently incapable of seeing their "real" (community) interest, but are guided exclusively by the desiderata of short-run gains. Indeed, the nation-state system is part of the problem, not of the solution. Thus, to ameliorate the problems on the agenda requires much more than mere institutional tinkering with the United Nations and its specialized agencies. Action is required to change human values, reduce global inequality, enhance the growth of transnational perspectives, develop global management capabilities, and ultimately to locate pathways for transcending the nation-state system. According to Mendlowitz there are already signs that this is occurring. "Today we may be in the throes of an ... epochal change—away from particularistically based territorial settlements serving a variety of agro-industrial units upon which the nation-state system was based, on to a truly global society with a global economy and global culture, and involving global governance" (1977, 261). If that epochal change comes to fruition, the Stoic ideal will have been achieved.

If the WOMP problematic is fairly explicit, though very broad, other efforts to create a global society paradigm are reticent in stating clearly what it is we ought to be studying or why. John Burton's spiderweb network of transactions and interconnections may be an apt portrayal (but only one) of the world, but like the advocates of international politics as transnational relations, it establishes no criteria for a focus, a raison d'être. There is no single problem or set of problems that this approach is supposed to illuminate, explain, or solve. The proponents of these approaches appear to be more intent on arguing the inadequacies of the classical paradigm than in showing what the proposed alternatives can or should do. A global society model which posits individuals and transnational organizations, and the processing of global issues, as the appropriate actors and units of analysis could lead the investigator to study anything from the International Ice Hockey Federation to the "diplomatic" relations between Montana and Manitoba. If there is a set of transactions that has some impact, or elicits some type of response from an actor in another area of the world, it becomes a legitimate phenomenon to study.

Both the classical tradition and the WOMP models are rooted in normative concerns; we are asked to study war and the large agenda of WOMP problems because there is ultimately some hope that increased knowledge will lead to greater political wisdom, at least, if not to total solutions. The other versions of the global society model do not have a similar focus, an animating concern; their proponents implicitly argue that it is sufficient to describe unique types of actors, their transactions and actions, and the bargaining over issue areas—no matter what their import.

Rosenau's concept of aggregation processes in a growing global community does not suffer equally from the lack of a problematic, although it is a rather particular one. He calls for the analysis of a "post-national order" (1980, 59) that is replete with significant changes, among them growing interdependence defined as an event or trend in one locale having some impact on another locale. Examples include a new technique of non-violent protest in Bombay being emulated in Oakland, California, or a speech in Israel's Knesset creating an uplifting experience in Boise, Idaho (p. 113). The purpose of mapping such processes of diffusion is not so much to shed light on a problem in the sense of war, peace, order, or pollution, but to develop a better understanding of the *dynamics of global change* and "thereby to trace new causal sources and possibly new parameters within which the course of events unfolds" (p. 5).

However, it is not just new types of events that are of theoretical importance—although in emphasizing them repeatedly, Rosenau may lead the reader astray. Foremost among the profound changes that appear to be taking place, in his view, is the growth of authority structures transcending national boundaries, structures that compete with the traditional loyalties directed to the nation state. Hence Rosenau's underlying problematic is to *describe and analyze the processes by which a genuine global community is being formed*—Kant's problem revisited, as it were, but without the normative dimension of overcoming war. Succinctly, Rosenau's problematic can be termed the *causes of systemic transformation, and the conditions for global community.* "The importance of nation-states relative to other actors undergoes noteworthy change when non-governmental, transnational, superordinate-subordinate relationships multiply to the extent that the directives issued by the other actors often evoke habitual compliance against the wishes of those who wield authority on behalf of the nation-states" (1980, 25). The analytical problem, then, appears to be something akin to the medieval struggles for loyalty between church and state, but with a more elaborate set of players. While some of the "new" elements of Rosenau's world view are rather suspect, at least he has delineated a problem area—global social change—that is intriguing and probably important. It is based, of course, on his conviction that the processes and character of change today are qualitatively and quantitatively different from those in previous eras, a proposition yet to be confirmed.

The operational-research difficulty with the problematic, however, is the same as with some of the other models of global society or transnational relations: given the units of analysis— transactions and aggregation that have impact across national boundaries—how is it possible to isolate the important actors and transactions from mundane and theoretically insignificant ones? The whole, massive web of transborder interactions becomes the analyst's field of research; there are no guidelines indicating where to begin or stop.

The second criterion, the units of analysis/essential actors, has already been introduced above. World society modelers share a theoretical and normative disdain for the nation state and the states system. Diplomatic-strategic behavior is not the essential area for inquiry, although why this should be so is not always clear. The field of international theory has to be broadened extensively to include study of all actors and the processes they engage in, which contribute to the problems of hunger, disease, war, inequality, human rights violations, and the like, and the ways which can help alleviate them. The units of analysis are similarly broadened into a global society and/or the specific issues under review.

For Rosenau, the analytical units are "aggregations," or aggregative/disaggregative processes which can, conceptually, take place at any level of social organization. "The key to making a full break with the differentiated state paradigm and constructing new ones ... lies in the readiness to treat all collectivities as susceptible either to aggregative processes that transform them into larger wholes or to disaggregative processes that transform them from wholes into parts. For these processes are nothing less than the causal flows in international relations" (1980, 145). Compared to diplomatic-strategic behaviors and processes as units of analysis, the notion of aggregative/disaggregative activities is much more abstract and can include an immense variety of actors. But the starting point is always the activities of individuals.

The images of the world in the global society models derive primarily from the evidence of growing "interdependence." The standard position is that trade, technology, communications, tourism, and the vast network of transnational relationships between private citizens, associations, and companies has reached a point of such density that today there is already the framework of a world society based on a global economy. Numerous studies have charted the growth of economic contacts between societies, the rise of international nongovernmental organizations, unprecedented levels of transboundary currency transactions, and the multifarious activities of global corporations, massive economic units which see the entire world, including the socialist economies, as their locus operandi. For them, national frontiers and regulations constitute only inconveniences to be circumvented by transfer pricing, constructive tax evasion, and three-way trade; if such devices do not work, a productive unit can simply be moved elsewhere. No society is immune to the economic tides of expansion and recession, and nationally determined policies seeking to create buffers against these tides are generally of little avail. Governments have lost control over financial flows—billions of dollars or any other currency can "leave" a country within minutes—so that one of the traditional instruments used by governments to regulate national economies has been lost to thousands of bankers, industrial firms, and currency speculators. Such loss of national control over the levers of domestic economic policy perhaps symbolizes the new world: authority structures of sovereign states have become compromised with the result that national societies and economies suffer from unprecedented vulnerabilities. The conclusion from these trends, of course, is that global problems require global solutions. A world economy in recession cannot be bailed out by one government practising strict monetarist policies while another pursues policies of Keynesian economic stimulation. At a minimum, the coordination of national policies is essential.

Associated with the growth of economic interdependence is the slow but inexorable process of developing a global society in the realms of personal contact and value systems. This can be measured in a number of ways, but most studies rely on the evidence of sensational increases in personal contacts across national frontiers: tourism, mail flows, international academic, business, and religious conferences; international sports events; the spreading use of English as a lingua franca, and the like.[2] Where personal contacts are not involved, communications technologies have enabled people to be dramatically more aware of each other. An event in a remote area of the world becomes a global event. The phenomenon of the "international demonstration effect" constitutes one of the many dimensions of change noted by Rosenau and many others: a new fact, political modus operandi (such as skyjacking), or ideological innovation is quickly disseminated around the world, and governments are unable to control them. Jazz, jeans, and premarital sex are the bane of the "new Soviet man" just as much as they are of religious fundamentalists and others in the West or Asia. There is thus plenty of evidence indicating a trend toward a universal society and popular culture. More important, perhaps, is the considerable evidence, marshaled by Alex Inkeles (1981) and others, that social structures and institutions are also converging throughout the world: extended families are being replaced by Western-style nuclear families; the large spreads in life expectancy that were typical of the North-South cleavage in the early postwar years are beginning to decline; social welfare policies around the world are becoming increasingly copies of each other. There are many indicators of social convergence, and they all point in the direction of increased cultural and institutional similarity. National differences are diminishing in the face of strong technological, socioeconomic pressures toward uniformity; national ramparts constructed to preserve traditions ultimately give way to the processes of universal homogenization.

In brief, the various images of the world come to a single conclusion: one world, ever "shrinking," and if not yet a true global society in moral and value terms, the trend is toward that direction. This is a world fundamentally different from the states system portrayed in the writings of the classical theorists and most of their modern successors. Given the changes that have occurred in the social, communications, and economic domains, to speak of a world of nation states, each more or less sealed off from the others, with interconnections between them limited mostly to the activities of diplomats, warriors, and a few commercial agents, no longer makes sense. The nation-state paradigm is so at odds with the empirical and normative realities of today that it must be replaced by models that incorporate the various changes, trends, and processes outlined above.[3]

Critique of the Classical Paradigm

Because of the discontinuity between the global society modelers' images of the world and those of the classical tradition, the proponents of the former have elaborated strong critiques against the classical tradition, particularly denouncing the "realist" school of American scholarship in international politics. Each has its own emphases in terms of the empirical and normative inadequacies of "realism," but perhaps the most comprehensive and fundamental catalogue of theoretical deficiencies has been outlined by Charles R. Beitz who, for our purposes, can represent the others.[4]

Beitz claims that international theory in the Anglo-American tradition has adhered to a Hobbesian view of "international skepticism" (1979, 36) which is synonymous with the lack of trust that leads to the "state of war." For this characterization of international politics to be accurate, according to Beitz, four conditions have to be met—and contemporary global conditions suggest that none of them can be met. First, the essential actors in international politics are states—and only states. Second, there is a rough equality of power among the actors, in the sense that the weakest can defeat the strongest. Third, the states are relatively impermeable, and thus formulate their own domestic policies; domestic and international politics are different realms of action, operating under fundamentally different rules of the game. Fourth, the essential characteristic of the states system is the lack of international authority, and hence there can be no expectations of reciprocal compliance in agreements made by

54

states (p. 36). While Beitz has perhaps set up a straw man in the sense that very few of the "realists," including Morgenthau, have adhered faithfully to all these assumptions (nor did Hobbes, it might be added), the categories are useful in summarizing the main points in the critique of the classical paradigm.

Virtually all the works labeled here as world or global society models—and many others—have noted the unwillingness of "realists" to acknowledge the importance of nonstate actors. The profusion and proliferation of nongovernmental international organizations, multinational corporations, global lobby groups, and the like *do* have an impact on states' foreign policies, and in many cases they create an international agenda of issues that must be dealt with, whether governments like it or not. Other nonstate actors like the Palestine Liberation Organization even have the potential of creating war and peace. The global society models, they claim, have the virtue of not prejudging the issue: the actors are those who initiate, bargain, set agendas, and resolve global and regional issues. They may be states, but they may also be a combination of actors that have only tangential connections to states. Who, for example, could adequately explain the international "outcome" of whaling moratoria without analyzing the activities of environmental groups manned by citizens from a variety of countries?

Second, there is no rough equality among state actors. The power disparity between the Super Powers and the micro states today is infinitely greater than was the difference, for example, between France and Mecklenburg-Schwerin in the eighteenth century. Contemporary relationships between the weak and the strong are characterized by dependency and asymmetrical vulnerability, not by rough parity. The weak, unless they develop nuclear capabilities, have no capacity to harm the strong in any meaningful way—except perhaps through coalitions such as OPEC.

Third, that states are no longer independent of each other hardly needs elaboration. The old dichotomy between domestic and foreign policy has broken down. Every state is more or less penetrated by foreign agents, and various linkages between the domestic politics of one state and the foreign policy interests of others are profuse and growing. One does not have to look further than Washington, D.C., where hundreds of lobbyists are registered as agents of foreign powers; or to El Salvador, Vietnam, Afghanistan, and elsewhere to realize the extent of the breakdown of the domestic–foriegn policy distinction. The latter cases illustrate compellingly the extent to which many regimes are only conditionally viable; they cannot even *exist* without foreign support. Hobbes and Rousseau, writing in an age when the notion of sovereignty coincided with the facts of politics, were not familiar with such phenomena. Moreover, as suggested above, most governments today have lost a good deal of their former freedom of choice in formulating domestic politics. International trends or asymmetrical dependencies require governments to coordinate their policies with those of others—even when it is not in their interest to do so. Interest rates in Canada, to take just one example, must fluctuate within a percentage or less of the American rates; if they are significantly lower than those in America, a massive outflow of funds would result, leaving Canada with capital and other types of crises. The kings and princes of eighteenth- and nineteenth-century Europe faced no similar constraints.

Finally, and perhaps broadening Beitz's last category somewhat, the proponents of the global society paradigm fault the "realists" for placing an undue emphasis on the search for power, a view of international politics that denies the existence of common interests and which directs research and teaching exclusively to the phenomenon of conflict. The classical perspective conditions us to examine only that which emanates from an assumption of man as essentially evil: the lust for power, the lack of harmony among peoples and states, the constant alert for threats rather than joint opportunities, the lack of trust, and the emphasis on self-help.[5] Reality, of course, is much more complicated. A global society model acknowledges, first, no constant human nature, although there is a human community with common needs and aspirations. Second, it points to the multitude of contacts between states and nonstate actors where cooperation leads to joint value-maximization. Third, it argues that there is no endless, repetitive power politics game; man can, and has learned, and in any case many strategies of power maximization today would lead to a situation where everyone ends up worse off. In a finite, interdependent global system, the excessive gains of one may be sufficient to destroy the whole system, including the actor seeking to maximize its advantage. Finally, many have noted that the classical perspective assumes power maximization in terms of territorial expansion. But today, the index of power is no longer territorial expanse, but technological, economic, and military-weaponry leadership—

combined perhaps with some moral leadership as well. Governments, according to Puchala and Fagan, are "increasingly absorbed in enhancing the economic, social, and intellectual well-being of their citizens via their foreign policies and international interactions" (1974, 249). The old power game of Rousseau's world does not fit the requirements of these new types of social welfare goals. To pursue them in a Hobbesian fashion in an age of interdependence would bring only unwanted consequences.

To complete the critique of realism, the world society modelers would add a fifth category to Beitz's roster: the realist school's limited problematic. While war remains a central problem, the virtue of a more "holistic"[6] perspective is that it identifies the interconnectedness of problems, a most important consequence of interdependence. According to Falk, in the old order problems were not so interconnected; hence it was possible to examine them using concepts appropriate to each. But present threats to human existence, ranging from war to environmental degradation, "are interconnected and cannot be successfully treated as separate and separable. ... If the subject matter of International Relations is extended [to include a variety of problems] then it is clear that concepts associated with the state-centric perspective ... have very little relevance. You cannot deter, balance or form an alliance against environmental decay" (Falk 1971, 98). From the point of view of the classical tradition, perhaps this last line of criticism is the most crucial, because to remedy the realists' shortcoming requires more than mere adjustments in the theoretical perspectives on actors, system, and processes; it virtually redefines the field of study.

Meddling or Modeling?

Despite some of the trenchant criticisms leveled against the "realist" school—though the characterization of the "realists" is completely accurate neither in terms of the contemporary study of international politics, nor in terms of the understanding of Hobbes—some of the global society modelers reveal ambiguities in their commitment to a fundamentally new paradigm. The stubborn facts of international life—economic equivalents of wars, the inability or unwillingness of governments to relinquish short-term gains for long-term community benefits—

continue to persist. How does one deal with these uncomfortable facts?

In the case of issue-area processes, as elaborated by Mansbach and Vasquez (1981), the procedure is theoretically to demolish the state-centric paradigm, only to reconstruct it in the empirical studies of issue areas. Various actors (not just governments) are involved in these issues, as they go through an issue cycle. But not unexpectedly, in their case studies, almost all the actors are in fact governments or *their agents*. The search for theoretical novelty thus ends up with a serious case—using Rosenau's term—of meddling rather than modeling: There is nothing inherent in any of the classical versions of international politics that precludes disaggregating foreign policy into separate issue compartments, or states into decision-makers. While Rousseau, for example, spoke of war and conflicts, the latter concept did not theoretically exclude commercial relations and other policy domains (Hoffmann 1965, 85).[7] Adding a few nonstate actors such as the Viet Cong (and they were certainly agents of the governing party in North Vietnam) to the "Vietnam Issue" does not compromise the utility of the classical paradigm. How theoretically advantageous an issue-area approach is compared to a traditional analysis of diplomatic-strategic behavior is not very clear.

Rosenau, while explicitly committed to modeling ("I . . . fully subscribe to the transformation [of world politics] assumption" [1980, 83]), notes, however reluctantly, that "nation states and their governments continue to be centers of decision and prime movers in the affairs of men" (p.113). In his research on the creation of the NIEO agenda, he finds little reported evidence of the demand aggregative process—the activities of micro units—that is not in fact government policy. (It could also be argued that the appropriate way to study the development of the NIEO or any other global issue is *not* to use events data. A little old-fashioned research might have provided the evidence of aggregative processes Rosenau was seeking.) Thus, while concepts such as micro units, aggregation, and macro units might prove useful in unraveling the history of various issues and how they eventually emerge on the international agenda, there is no extensive body of evidence to suggest that the issues of true global importance will be achieved through any means other than state diplomatic bargaining, the construction of intergovernmental coalitions, the exertions of diplomatic and economic pressures and rewards, and perhaps the threat or use of force—that is, through structures and processes akin to those specified in the classical paradigm.

The WOMP models are perhaps the closest to genuine modeling because of their heavy emphasis on new units of analysis (the global society and its processes), their images of the world as essentially composed of individuals and collectivities of individuals other than states, and their view that there *is* an objective global community interest separable from and inconsistent with the interests of states.[8] This latter view represents a particularly important break from the classical tradition and belongs squarely among the conceptualizations developed by the Stoics, medieval thinkers, and Kant—a cosmopolitan human community.

Other efforts to operationalize world society models seem compelled in research to return to the activities of states, through their governments and agents, because of political scientists' long-standing commitment to the positivist tradition which requires an emphasis on critical realities and on attempts to understand and explain them. The WOMP models, in contrast, are constructed to illuminate the paths that will transcend present realities. They are turned toward the future, with present realities not much hindrance to creative imagination.

It is one thing to chart change such as increasing interdependence and growth in the variety of actors, but another to argue compellingly that the logical consequence of this type of change is a fundamentally new type of international politics, requiring new models to comprehend its inner dynamics. While the non-WOMP models of the global society undoubtedly have intellectual merits, as we shall point out in the concluding chapter, the work to date suggests the ubiquitous impact of states and the continued importance of the states system. There has been interesting modeling at the theoretical level, but in empirical research, meddling seems to predominate. The addition of novel types of actors or the delineation of greater complexity in international processes have not conclusively demonstrated a radical transformation in the logic of diplomatic–strategic behaviour (cf. Hoffmann 1978, 109).

In sum, the global society paradigm constitutes only a modest challenge to the classical tradition. While some of the critiques of the realist tradition are trenchant, the theoretical and empirical work to date has not established the persuasiveness of organizing the field around an alternative paradigm. Some of the efforts lack a clear problematic; others, such as many WOMP formulations, expand the problematic so broadly that it is impossible to develop guidelines and priorities for research. The emphasis on shifting to different units of analysis/actors, in the context of a global community, has not paid off handsomely. Too much of the real world of international politics continues to take place among the traditional state actors operating in a states system, searching for stability and order sometimes, but more often pursuing their short-run interests in the manner described by Hobbes, Rousseau, and their modern successors.

Notes: Chapter 3

1 Representative works would include: Falk 1971; Brown 1972; Sprout and Sprout 1971; Beres and Targ 1975; Mische and Mische 1977; Kothari 1974.
2 For example, see the statement by Alex Inkeles (1975).
3 Few have come to the defense of the states system as a form of organizing the world that brings numerous social, economic, and cultural benefits. An interesting argument that international pluralism brings such benefits is Robert G. Wesson's *State Systems* (1978). I have presented an argument against too much "interconnectedness" in Holsti 1975.
4 Beitz is not to my knowledge associated with any of the world society models discussed above. I use his work only because it contains a succinct and reasonably comprehensive critique of the "realist" tradition.
5 For another critique of the "power politics" school, see Taylor 1978b.
6 The term is used in Little 1978 (p. 197).
7 In this work Hoffmann demonstrates how a Rousseau-type analysis could be used to examine the EEC.
8 Not all WOMP models share this view with equal conviction. Rajni Kothari, for example, argues that there can be no movement toward a just world community until presently exploited LDCs gain genuine autonomy and a modicum of equality *as states* (Kothari 1974).

4

Neo-Marxist Challenges to the Classical Tradition

In the case of the application of Marxist method, an exciting impetus is provided with the identification of class as a transnational actor, and the concept of class struggle as the identification and resolution of contradictions in society as providing the dynamic. Through this is seen a world divided not into states but into class antagonisms and a dichotomy of riches and poverty, with imperialism and economic and political asymmetrical penetration affecting the fortunes of millions of people. ... What it ultimately amounts to is that Marxism is fundamentally revolutionary in terms of international relations ... because ... it does not accept the traditional state-centric model of world politics. ... It is this denial of the primacy of the state that puts the Marxist perspective into a category of its own. (Thorndike 1978, 56)

Although Marx and some of his disciples shared with the global society theorists the ultimate vision of a universal social order transcending the nation-state system, they and the form of inquiry they founded had little impact until recently on the field of international politics and theory. The names of Marx, Engels, Lenin, or other prominent figures in the tradition seldom appear in the literature of the field. Historical materialism, the dialectic method, and class analysis were relevant to analyzing the dynamics of change in societies reeling from the impact of industrialization, but aside from colonialism they had little to add to the incisive writings of Hobbes, Grotius, Rousseau, and

61

others when it came to the problem of relations between states. This is not to say that Marx and his successors were unconcerned about the problems of peace and war; but what they said was open to challenge on numerous grounds, not the least of which was that they could not seem to make up their own minds on some critical matters. Marx, and particularly Engels, who had been a keen observer of military affairs during the American Civil War and during the late nineteenth century in Europe, were understandably more preoccupied with outlining ways to transform domestic societies than with developing a systematic theory of international politics. Moreover, in one interpretation of their views, war is a social problem, a manifestation of the capitalist system; it cannot be dealt with on the political level until the victory of the proletariat has been secured. Gallie reminds us, also, that while Marx and Engels were at the height of their intellectual development, Europe was enjoying a period of relative diplomatic calm, so that the problem which had been foremost in the minds of Rousseau and Kant was not of equally compelling importance during the era of the Concert of Europe (Gallie 1978, 78–9). We should recall finally that the eighteenth-century philosophers' concern about war was not based solely on humanitarian grounds; they condemned war as a major impediment to political reform and democratization. Republicanism, however, had triumphed throughout most of Europe by 1871, whereas the plight of the proletariat was an object of continuing social concern. Marxism, in whatever variant, is ultimately concerned with the problems of modernization, exploitation, and inequality; these are the endemic, pervasive, and seemingly perpetual problems, while war in the nineteenth century was sporadic and, by today's standards, relatively brief and of limited destructiveness. The critical social issue of the latter part of the nineteenth century was the relationship between capital and labor, not the one between the diplomats and warriors of the several states.

It is perhaps for these reasons that most of the important modern contributors to international theory, themselves often qualified experts on Marxism (E. H. Carr, for example), have not relied on Marxist insights in their own contributions to the field. The vast output of theoretically relevant literature emanating from the "behavioral revolution" was similarly uninfluenced by the numerous branches of Marxist thought. Even the modern Marxist interpreters, such as Baran, Althusser, and Gramsci, are seldom cited in the literature of the field.

Since the late 1960s, however, the pages of academic international relations journals and the meetings of professional societies have become inundated with the writings and lectures of those who offer a new (and presumably more accurate, as Thorndike's comments suggest) perspective on international relations, one that borrows from Marx such notions as dialectical processes, the determining influence of economic structures, social contradictions, and the overriding normative concern with exploitation, domination, and dependence at the international level. These are the numerous versions of "dependency theory" and "world capitalist-system" theory.

The differences that divide tendencies within these two formulations may be as important as the common assumptions that unite them,[1] but since our task is not to evaluate the theories as contributions to knowledge, but to examine how they relate to teaching and research in international politics and theory, we will deal with them as a single corpus of thought that extends to the analysis of the contemporary international scene many ideas and concepts developed by Marx. Both theories, which operate essentially within a single paradigm, also introduce important new insights: they are beholden to Marx, but are in many ways creative and original. Our points of reference will be the major works by authors such as Paul Baran, Andre Gunder Frank, Fernando Cardoso and Enzo Faletto, Samir Amin, Johan Galtung, and Immanuel Wallerstein.

Since the remarks that follow tend to be critical, in the sense that the dependency/world capitalist-system paradigm does not successfully challenge the traditional approach to international theory, it is necessary first to absolve those authors from purposes or intellectual claims which they have not made. They are basically concerned with the problem of underdevelopment and, to my knowledge, none has asserted that the neo-Marxist paradigm (the term we will use in the following pages) is designed to replace, or even to supplement the traditional concerns of international politics scholars. The claims to the equal usefulness of the two paradigms, to the necessity for synthesis between them, or even to the predominance or superiority of the neo-Marxist paradigm for the study of international politics come mostly from political scientists whose prior work has been within the classical tradition. Statements of this sort have been made, for example, by Ralph Pettman (1979, esp. p. 65), who urges synthesis, by the editors of a special issue of the *International Studies Quarterly*, W. Ladd Hollist and James Rosenau (also synthetists), and by Tony Thorndike (1978) and the sociologist Christopher Chase-Dunn (1981),[2] who in effect argue the superiority of the neo-Marxist paradigm.

Marx and the Neo-Marxist Paradigm:
Some Essential Differences

Marx

Marx was seriously interested in non-European societies, wrote extensively about "oriental despotism," and made a specialty of Indian studies. In regarding the hopes for the future of these societies, he was an optimist because, in his view, only capitalism as a mode of production brings development; and as the connection between Europe and these areas became richer, capitalism would replace precapitalist economic forms.

Capitalism does not develop evenly around the world. It emerges initially in a few cores and as these accumulate wealth it spreads laterally, eventually engulfing the globe. This process was to be applauded, not just because it was a necessary precondition for proletarian revolution, but also because it would bring undoubted material benefits to millions of people languishing in stagnant precapitalist economies, enjoying none of the fruits of technological and scientific progress. Marx's view of the spread of capitalism did not portray the cores exploiting the non-European hinterlands; the historical development of capitalism was not a zero-sum game between industrial and preindustrial societies. Through its lateral spread, everyone benefited—at least initially (Brewer 1980, 17). In any case, Marx did not attribute the economic backwardness of the non-European regions to capitalism, since most of those areas had remained relatively isolated from a meaningful commercial nexus until the late nineteenth century.

Lenin shared Marx's optimism and predicted that increasingly the centers of production would shift to the colonial areas as wage rates and other factors of production there would become increasingly advantageous. If anything, it was the industrial centers of the world that would stagnate. In *Imperialism, the Highest Stage of Capitalism* (1939) Lenin painted a glowing portrait of the long-range economic prospects for the colonial areas. While the spread of capitalism was uneven, its ultimate domination would lead to uniformity in methods of production and standards of living. Capitalism expands wealth, at least absolutely if not relatively. Neither Marx nor Lenin hypothesized that

64

the consequences of capitalism's spread to the colonial areas would be different from those observed in the industrializing societies of Europe and North America.

The neo-Marxist paradigm borrows a great deal from classical Marxism, including the dialectical method, historical materialism, classes as essential actors, the creative and progressive opportunities offered by social conflict, and a system-dominant perspective which explains typical patterns of actor behavior by the structure of economic modes of production. But where it diverges fundamentally is in the view of the role and future of the colonial and postcolonial lands in the world capitalist system. As A. G. Frank has put it, underdevelopment is the reverse of the development coin. The development of the core "undevelops" the periphery. Whereas Marx and Lenin were optimistic about the consequences of the spread of capitalism to what is now termed the Third World, the neo-Marxists are fundamentally pessimistic.

Paul Baran, in his *Political Economy of Growth* (1957), inaugurated this important shift by suggesting that the developing countries would undergo economic processes *different* from those which the industrial nations had experienced in the nineteenth century and earlier. He viewed the world as having essentially a fixed income, over which there is a struggle for shares; hence, the relationship between rich and poor at the international level is characterized by a zero-sum situation. In later works by Frank, Amin, Galtung, Wallerstein, and others, *qualitative* differences between center and periphery become enshrined as cornerstones of their world images. *A* and *B* can never be equal because they perform fundamentally different functions in the capitalist world system, the one growing, innovating technologically, and exploiting, the other stagnating, undeveloping as the result of the outward flow of surplus capital, and providing cheap commodities for the center. There can be no justice or equality in the world, much less meaningful economic development in the peripheries of such a global system, with such fixed roles and structures.

The Neo-Marxist Problematic

While there are such important differences between classical Marxism and the newer formulations regarding the role and nature of capitalism in global development, they share a common moral concern with exploitation. The problematic of the new neo-Marxist paradigm is *the causes of inequality/exploitation and the conditions for equality, and in some versions, for political and economic autonomy.* As we will argue below, the question of war and peace is only of peripheral interest, while on the question of order there is a fundamental incompatibility between the classical tradition and the neo-Marxist paradigm.

The neo-Marxist paradigm did not emerge from dissatisfaction with the study of international politics. It was, rather, a response to the theories of economic development that had informed both inquiry and policy during the 1950s and 1960s. The conventional economic wisdom of that era proposed that development would be achieved through a mixture of export-led industrialization, sound taxation policies, private foreign investment, and foreign aid. The barriers to development, Western economists argued, resided primarily within the countries themselves; these included such social and cultural phenomena as the extended family, religious practices, patterns of landholding, lack of capital, and rational economic decision-making, as well as political obstacles such as corruption, regime instability, and inefficient bureaucracies. Development would thus require vast social reforms as well as sound economic strategies.

A number of Latin American economists, sociologists, and historians rejected these conventional recipes for development and modernization, along with the ahistorical and positivist methodologies that had been employed in developing the appropriate economic theories. They suggested instead that their nations cannot go individually through "stages" of development when they are merely a part of a world capitalist system that fundamentally conditions the paths of economic change.[3] There can be no autonomous development, maximizing gains for an underdeveloped society, when the economies of these countries have been organized via colonialism, and remain today, to serve the interests of the metropolitan powers. The barriers to development are not internal, as liberal Western economists would have it, but derive from the structural characteristics of the global capitalist system, from the functional differentiation that occurred during the worldwide spread of capitalism. Hence, to talk of "national" development programs makes no sense since the persisting international structures vastly limit the range of national choice. The system is all-predominant, and its needs must be served rather than those of any component units.

The basic result of the operation of the world capitalist system is global economic inequality. Different authors posit different exploitative devices (although they do not always bother to define exploitation), but all agree that the processes leading to these consequences involve the draining of surplus value from the poor societies to the rich, from the peripheries to the center. The unequal exchange between center and periphery has been historically determined, through the expansion of European capitalism and the search for raw materials. This expansion was not a spontaneous "explosion" of capitalist activity worldwide, but was directed from the centre, to serve its own needs. In Wallerstein's view (1974, 162), "the capitalist world-economy was built on a worldwide division of labor in which various zones of this economy [core, semi-periphery, and periphery] were assigned specific economic roles, developed different class structures, used consequently different modes of labor control, and profited unequally from the workings of the system." Crucial to this concept of differing—and unequal—roles is the view of the division of labor, which Wallerstein (1979, 14–15) defines as a "grid which is substantially interdependent. Economic actors operate on ... assumption ... that the totality of their essential needs—of sustenance, protection and pleasure—will be met over a reasonable time span by a combination of their own productive activities and exchange in some form. ... Both exchange partners can reap windfalls simultaneously but only one can obtain maximum profit, since the exchange of surplus value within a system is a zero-sum game."

It is not clear why the exchange is inherently zero-sum, particularly since Wallerstein acknowledges a variable sum situation when both partners can jointly reap windfalls. Nevertheless, most *dependencia* and world capitalist-system theories assume the zero-sum characteristic of economic exchange and for this reason share Marx's normative concerns. The sources of inequality are the objects of study, and equality is the goal of practical action deriving from historical and sociological analysis.[4]

The Nature of Actors and Units of Analysis

The unit of analysis is in most versions of the theories under consideration the world capitalist system, or for some, the exchange process. All actions and exchanges take place within the system. According to Wallerstein, there can be no significant structural change in national societies unless there is change in the system as a whole. (This view raises a number of logical and political difficulties, not to mention debates among various authors.) Hence, even the socialist states today are part of the world capitalist system, and presumably suffer as a result. No peripheral country can solve its problems, that is, avoid exploitation, merely by undergoing a socialist revolution. There has to be a system-wide transformation, from a world capitalist system to a global socialist system. Many *dependencia* figures, who in some cases are close to the centers of national decision-making, would seriously challenge this view. If the realm of action is substantially determined by system characteristics, how can the actors have any freedom of maneuver, how can local policies be geared at least to ameliorate the worst features of exploitation?

The solution is in the dialectic, in the notion of contradictions. To Cardoso and Faletto, for example, international structures do determine behavior and establish recurring patterns of exchange. However, "they also generate contradictions and social tensions, opening the possibility for [local] social movements and ideologies of change" (Cardoso and Faletto 1979, xi). There are, then, possibilities for alternatives in history. Opposing forces drag history ahead (or backward), but those forces should be seen in a global context, not as mere local groupings responding only to local conditions. Societies, classes, groups, and organizations, no matter what the conceptualized actor, do not have parallel or separate histories, but are parts of the whole, reflecting the whole (Wallerstein 1979, 53). Thus, unlike the state-as-actor approach of the classical international politics paradigm, where recurrence, repetition, and lack of change are characteristic of world politics (arms races, balancing of power, alliances, and the like are observed in ancient international systems as well as today), in the neo-Marxist formulations the actors may be agents of qualitative change toward fundamentally new structures and processes.

Some political scientists have adopted the dependency/world capitalist-system paradigm not because of any commitment to the dialectical method, sudden conversion to an interest in history, or fascination with economics, but rather because it frees them from viewing the field only in terms of the overt actions of states. In the Marxist view, states are only derivative; the real actors—those that bring change and affect the lives of the people (not just diplomats and warriors)—are classes and various class-based transnational associations. Hence in his praise for the uncompromisingly "internationalist" outlook of Marx and his successors, Thorndike (1978, 70) suggests that the appropriate actors to study are transnational working class and associated revolutionary movements, and national liberal movements; the most important issues for study include multinational corporations, transnational financial flows, and economic dependency. Thorndike suggests that this agenda for research "does not deny the validity of other issues, but ... they too can be viewed through the analytical framework presented by the [Marxist] paradigm" (p. 80). Like most others, though, he does not show how the paradigm can shed light on the traditional questions of international theory.

But the state cannot simply disappear, or be passed off as a mere handmaiden of economic interests, if there is to be any meaningful analysis of international politics. The troublesome ubiquity of the state has given rise to virtually a new intellectual industry: exploring the nexus between class-based organizations and the state. Wallerstein's writings, among others, have been an important fillip to this issue. Because his historical analysis largely ignores the domain of politics and diplomacy, and characterizes the state as little more than the protector of dominant economic groups, he has generated strong criticism (cf. Zolberg 1981).[5] To help reduce this point of vulnerability, recent literature in the dependency/world capitalist-system frameworks has sought to explore the relationship between economics and politics (Chase-Dunn 1981).[6] The debate has hardly been settled, but it reveals some discomfort among the adherents of the neo-Marxist paradigm in viewing the world of international politics from the perspective of class actors and units of analysis based solely on commercial exchange.

Guidance on this question does not come from Soviet scholars either. Russian theorists have been equally bedevilled by the problem. On the one hand, they analyze international politics from the point of view of class conflict, contradictions, "progressive" and "reactionary" forces, the nature of imperialism, and the proletariat as the carrier of historical progress, relegating the state to an instrument of the ruling class. On the other hand, they face important theoretical difficulties when they analyze the variety of regimes whose pedigree is neither bourgeois nor socialist, or societies that bear little resemblance to those of Europe in Marx's time, when they see wars that have nothing to do with imperialism, or when they continually defend the critical importance of Soviet sovereignty, a concept which Marx sought to demolish with his notion that the workers have no homeland. Thus, while numerous authors have insisted on the critical importance of nonstate actors and exchange processes in any relationships which could be termed "international," their analyses usually end up with a focus on the actions and interactions of states.[7] Despite the protestations of Cardoso and Faletto—to mention only two authors—that there is no such thing as dependency between *states* (1979, 173), the existing empirical work employing dependency theory has used the state or national economy almost exclusively as the unit of statistical and historical analysis.

As much as the proponents of the neo-Marxist paradigm have celebrated the importance of class and other nonstate actors in international politics, they have yet to make a persuasive case for this position. Those, like Wallerstein, who have genuinely adhered to an analytic scheme of economic primacy have had to weather devastating criticism. Those who have explored the connection between the merchant and the diplomat usually end up discussing the relations between states, or between major power organizations such as multinational corporations, and states. A further problem is empirical: a number of studies demonstrate that when state and commercial interests clash, the former usually prevail—even in relatively "weak" states. There are significant exceptions, of course, but they do not constitute sufficient numbers to support any generalization about the supposed supremacy of commercial imperatives.

Images of the World

Neo-Marxists are substantially unified in their depictions and diagnoses of the world of exchange, transnational relations, exploitation, and dependency, A basic characteristic of the world is distinct economic *functions*, those discrete and typical forms of production essentially unique to different regions, the centre, and the peripheries. Wallerstein adds the in-between category of semiperipheries, regions or states like Singapore which also play distinct economic roles in the global capitalist system. Historically there has been movement beween the semiperiphery and the centre (Spain and Portugal's decline to semiperiphery status, and the rise of Holland to the centre in the seventeenth century), but for a variety of reasons the peripheries have no possibility of becoming part of the centre so long as the present division of labor exists.

The peripheries are dependent upon the centre in the sense that their economic priorities and processes are not autonomously determined, but are a reflection of the center's policies and needs. The flow of surplus is upward to the center from the periphery, while the basic structure is maintained by a downward flow of instruments of control, including finance capital, foreign aid, cultural domination, alliances and military assistance, and, in extremis, subversion and intervention. States may be the agents under whose names the fundamental structures are maintained, but they are only the spokesmen of the true actors, the captains of industry and finance, and the multinational corporations.

Despite the bifurcation of the global capitalist system according to economic function, the world has become a single economic unit, an integrated system in which there are few if any pockets of the precapitalist order remaining. Only a few tribes in the jungles of the Congo or Borneo remain outside the system, and are of no analytical interest or political importance. Everything else is connected, meaning that there is no such thing as a disconnected "local" history or, for that matter, local development. Since the world system and its structures of exploitation are the foci of analysis, the preferred research agenda is the stages and development of the system rather than the history of particular social units within it.

The second critical characteristic of the neo-Marxist world image, after the notion of distinct economic functions, is scarcity. Every dynamic within the system is portrayed in zero-sum terms. Exchanges have winners and losers, not joint gainers; economies moving from the semiperiphery to the center do so at the expense not only of some members of the center, whom they replace, but also of others in the semiperipheries (Wallerstein 1979, 101). There can be no "global commons" of the type portrayed in the world society paradigm, because there is no such thing as a global interest. A class analysis (class being based on relationship to the means of production) presupposes conflicting interests between owners and workers; it also provides clues to distinguish progressive compared to reactionary forces. Given the ubiquitous nature of conflict within the world capitalist system—a point of similarity perhaps with the power politics vision in its most pessimistic (Rousseauian) form—there can never really be any meaningful or lasting social peace between actors, whether at the local, national, or international levels. What is good for the class-based economies of the centre necessarily reduces the welfare of the peripheries; increases in wealth in one arena are at the expense of wealth in others.

However, the theorists in question have little to say about the effects of *diminishing* wealth in the center, as during a depression. Logically, if, as in Frank's view, peripheral societies undevelop as a result of exchange with the center in good times, they should in fact develop during the bad times of the center. Frank in fact proposes that some Latin American countries experienced significant economic growth during the Great Depression and World War II, when the volume of transactions with the center declined considerably (Frank 1972). This may have been the case in the 1930s and 1940s, but all major postwar economic downturns in the center have produced little but drastically worsening conditions in the Third World. This fact alone suggests some flaws in the zero-sum characterization of the capitalist world system. And if the world is truly as depicted in the neo-Marxist paradigm, how does one explain the successful climb of some societies from essential poverty a generation ago to relative affluence today—a prediction made by Lenin? States such as Taiwan and South Korea are often depicted as unique or as exceptions. Even if there has been substantial development, there has been no decline in dependency or gain in economic and political autonomy. Other lines of explanation have also been advanced. But, in general, the proponents of the paradigm argue that those peripheries which seriously challenge the centers in terms of transforming assigned economic roles and functions will face the stringent application of the instruments of domination available to the center (Cardoso and Faletto 1979, 17). In other words, the international structures of the world capitalist system cannot through ordinary economic processes become more egalitarian. In the words of Cardoso and Faletto, "structures are based neither on egalitarian relationships nor on collaborative patterns of social organization. They are founded on social asymmetries and on exploitative types of social organizations" (p. x). This assertion is fundamental to the world view of the neo-Marxist paradigm.

The image of the world is thus profoundly pessimistic, as much so as the characterizations of Hobbes and Rouseau are in the domain of diplomacy and war. There are, to be sure, escape mechanisms in some versions, including revolution at the national level. But for the others, there is no solution to the problematic short of cataclysmic and sweeping change: the destruction of the world capitalist system and its replacement by global socialism. But the problem here is that there is no known model toward which to work, should capitalism be swept away.

The relations between present socialist states obviously do not offer a prototype for the future. No one could seriously claim that the mutal relations of the socialist states are devoid of dependency, exploitation, and domination, or that there is autonomy of decision-making in the most important realms of policy. The record of peace and war between the socialist states also provides no basis for enthusiasm (cf. Holsti 1980b). Hence, the ultimate transformation of the world is toward an unknown quality, a system which must have none of the features of economic differentiation typical of the world capitalist system; that is, toward a system which has never yet existed except in the minds of some far-seeing theorists. Like the global society modelers, the neo-Marxists are long on diagnosis of present ills, but short on defining the characteristics of a world polity that would, in fact, produce an end to exploitation and inequality. Both seek to transcend the world as they see it; the first to get away from the nation state and habits of thought associated with it, the second to overcome capitalism. But how alternative systems would resolve the stated problematics is frustratingly vague.

Prospects for Synthesis of Competing Paradigms

There are some surface similarities between neo-Marxist formulations of international relations and some of the ideas prominent in the classical tradition. The notion of system-dominance comes to mind, which means that the actions of the main behavioral units are determined within fixed limits by system structure or processes. There is also the idea that single clusters of variables are sufficient to explain both persistence or changes in typical behavior. For the neo-Marxist, the international division of labor is sufficient; for classical international theory, the logic of state independence explains war, if not its variation. Although we have come a long way since the eighteenth century in acknowledging the importance of economic issues in diplomatic life, some formulations of power politics in this century were certainly shortsighted in confining explanations of endurance and change solely to power variables. Likewise, the neo-Marxists have been faulted for treating the political-diplomatic domain as a mere appendage of economic interests. In brief, the parallels between the paradigms help to highlight their one-dimensionality and to underscore some of their weaknesses. But surface similarities—particularly of weaknesses—provide no grounds for synthesis.

The only conclusion I can derive from reviewing the two literatures is that there is no possibility, and probably no desirability of synthesis. It is sufficient that the adherents of the two schools are aware of each other's existence and occasionally borrow insights from each other. (At the time of writing, it is clear that many political scientists have reviewed a good portion of the neo-Marxist literature, while the *dependencia* and some world capitalist-system originators seem mostly unfamiliar with the work of the major figures in international theory.)

The main reason for taking this position is that the two paradigms are concerned with fundamentally different problems, the one with peace, war, and order, the other with inequality, exploitation, and equality. The empirical connection between war and inequality remains problematic. Competing explanations of war that link it to nationalism, ethnic-language unity, secession, "national liberation," and fundamentally strategic issues (security) are far more numerous and persuasive. There is thus no more reason to seek synthesis between these two topics than there is for the dental researcher to integrate work with someone doing research on cancer of the colon. Because both study a human affliction is not sufficient reason to claim that the intellectual tools, concepts, and research agendas of the two should be integrated. There *may* be some connection between the afflictions, but present evidence suggests that other connections (for example, dental research with nutrition) are more fruitful. No one has yet made a persuasive argument that international relations scholars, with their unique concerns, are better off studying neo-Marxist world views than they are studying the works of psychologists, geographers, strategic experts, game theorists, or communications analysts. This is not to say that the neo-Marxist paradigm is irrelevant to international relations as a source of insight for undergraduates' education, as a corrective for some overly narrow world views, and as a means of sensitizing researchers to the importance of economics in international relations. But the lack of interest of the neo-Marxists in the war/peace/security and order question

What about Lenin?

renders their analyses peripheral to the traditional interests, to the core of the subject of international politics.

Marxism, War, and Peace

Because neo-Marxist approaches to international relations focus on the problem of development, the issues of war, peace, security, and order receive little attention. To the extent that they are discussed at all, they are portrayed primarily as the instrumentalities the center uses to combat revolutionary threats against the economic structures of imperialism. War and international order are basically epiphenomena of class interests, related to productive processes in the same fashion that the state, politics, the arts, and religions are part of Marx's "superstructure." Compared to economic processes, wars, or the diplomatic orders created to maintain economic stability, are neither major causes nor consequences of historical change, and hence are not worthy of major inquiry. (The comment would not apply, of course, to armed struggle against imperialism or to class warfare, which are of utmost importance.) Classical interstate war remains a marginal concern.

It is not clear why, even with the focus on development, neo-Marxists should be so little concerned with the question that forms the core of international theory. Marx, Engels, and Lenin had a good deal to say about the problem, but perhaps it is their ambivalence or shortcomings on the question that has prevented modern *dependencia* and world capitalist-system theorists from raising the question to a more prominent place. According to Gallie (1978, esp. pp. 68–78) the standard interpretation of Marx and Engels is that war is indeed a part of the superstructure, an effect of underlying changes in the ways societies organize their productive processes. But he also demonstrates, through a careful textual analysis of Marx's writings, that another interpretation is equally valid, namely, that *war can be a phenomenon independent of productive processes or class relations*. In other words, war is a consequence of the fact that the world is organized into distinct political communities; it has an explanatory logic independent of economics. (This view does not deny that wars have been used for class interests, as in the case where "reactionaries" resort to it to forestall domestic revolution, or that wars can create revolutionary opportunities. This latter problem received extensive treatment from Engels in particular—but he also dreaded the oncoming World War I which he saw not just as a revolutionary opportunity, but as a major disaster for *all* mankind.)

Lenin's thesis on war is more doctrinaire in the sense that only a single economic variable is used to explain the phenomenon. Unlike Marx, Lenin does not separate war from underlying economic processes. War between capitalist states is inevitable because of unavoidable contradictions within the economic arrangements of capitalist states, and the need to expand economic activities abroad. Once the world is carved up among the imperialist powers, there can be no more opportunities for unopposed expansion, and any attempted gains will always be at the expense of others. Hence, a sufficient condition for the outbreak of World War I, and presumably for all other wars, is development toward the highest stage of capitalism, imperialism. Alliances, secret diplomacy, arms racing, balancing of power, or secret treaties are not causes of war but mere reflections of the underlying processes of national economic expansion. States which have reached the highest stage of capitalism —imperialism—necessarily go to war. When, where, or how is unimportant; the general tendency to war is explained in his theory.

There is not much in this body of thought to provide guidelines for an intriguing or authoritative diagnosis of the traditional problematic of international theory. To acknowledge that wars may occur irrespective of class interests or underlying socioeconomic processes is only a nod in the direction of conventional wisdom. To say that war between capitalist states is inevitable is like saying that collisions between Ford automobiles are inevitable; but which is the critical variable? automobile or Ford? state or economy? The theory also fails to explain critical variation in war incidence between capitalist states, nor does it address the embarrassing question posed by the dismal record of warfare between socialist states. Collisions between Volkswagens seem to be inevitable as well. (One could perhaps argue that wars between socialist states are inevitable as long as they are embedded in the world capitalist system, in the expectation that in a world of socialist states there would be no wars. This is wishful thinking in the extreme.) War as opportunity for revolutionary activity takes us to the realm of political action, not to explanation.

In brief, while Marx and his immediate heirs paid considerable attention to the problem of war, their statements compared to

76

those found in the corpus of international theory, whether traditional or behavioral, are unimpressive. If we want our students
to learn something about the phenomenon of war, we are better
advised to have them start with Thucydides, Hobbes, Rousseau,
Morgenthau, Quincy Wright, North and Choucri, and many
others, and to refer to Marx and his heirs only if extra time per-
mits. Neo-Marxist writings might be useful for illuminating *some*
interventionary activities of the capitalist great powers,[8] but
overall there is little possibility for a useful, overall synthesis
between the paradigms if our objective is a reasonably comprehensive and scientifically competent analysis of war and
peace.

Other Impediments to Synthesis

The neo-Marxists' lack of interest in the core questions of international theory is not the only reason why synthesis is difficult
and probably inadvisable. Of at least equal importance are
fundamental differences in world views and methodology. For
example, is it possible or desirable to promote a synthesis
between world views that have diametrically opposed normative claims and ideals?

Among the fundamental concerns of the classical tradition
is the question of *order*, defined here as the creation of a
reasonably stable pattern of international relationships that sus-
tains the independence of the states of the system and enhances
their opportunities for achieving both security and welfare
goals. Such an order may be incompatible with the kind of maximalist view of international justice typical in neo-Marxist
thought, but it is based on the view that peace and stability, particularly in a nuclear age, must take precedence over values such
as equality for all, when and if the two are incompatible.[9] The
overriding concern is perpetuation of the system itself, which
means not only that sovereign political units will continue to
exist—and sometimes wars will be fought to make certain they
do continue to exist—but also that the world will be characterized by political, economic, cultural, religious, and national
diversity. The goal of order requires a diplomacy that seeks to
reduce levels of conflict between states, or at least to manage or
control them.

The Marxist view is fundamentally different. Conflict is not
only inevitable, but is to be celebrated because it is the main

77

engine of historical change. Contradictions cannot be papered over by mechanisms of "peaceful change" or "conflict resolution," and should not be. International theorists have viewed war and conflict of any kind as phenomena to be avoided or at least controlled; the Marxist position has traditionally been to promote them when it serves class interests. When the world is viewed as inherently unjust, structured in such a manner as to perpetuate exploitation and inequality, then how can one raise order, implying an obnoxious status quo, to a high priority? Change, revolution, and equality must take precedence over a desire for order and stability.

Given the class nature of all politics, one cannot expect the captains of the center to adopt palliatives in favor of the peripheries, because in the zero-sum game this can only be at their own expense. Lacking a notion of the common or global public good (which is implied in a notion of international order), there cannot be meaningful collaboration between center and periphery for the advantage of both. War and conflict that have as their goal the destruction of the present structures of domination and exploitation are thus to be applauded and fostered. When the present states system is transformed into a world socialist system, that will be the appropriate time to be concerned about order and controlling conflict.

There also remains the question of diversity, one that has perplexed both Soviet and non-communist Marxists for a long time. We can assume that if it is the purpose of political action to transcend the present system, one of whose characteristic features is political, social, and cultural diversity, any alternative system is not likely to foster those very national forms of pluralism which have been associated with capitalism. The notion of a world federation of socialist states, or a global worker's commonwealth, is not likely to appeal to international theorists who, dispite the problem of war, generally see multiple virtues in the pluralism of more than 150 separate political communities.

On the methodological level, there are numerous problems that militate against synthesis; some of them are probably intractable. An entire generation trained in historical, philosophical, and quantitative techniques cannot easily adapt to, much less employ, dialectic methods. Behavioral scientists, for example, are inclined to search for quantitative change, while the Hegelian tradition directs the search for qualitative change. Positivism is not a qualification for work in the research agenda of the neo-Marxist paradigm, as recent efforts have illustrated. North American and European political scientists' and sociologists' attempts to quantify and "test" the hypotheses contained in depenedency theory have been firmly rejected by the Latin American formulators of those theories. Researchers cannot explore "degrees of dependency" between states when classes are the crucial actors, and when dependency is built into the entire system. Nor does it make sense to elaborate statistical photos of a dependency relationship, when those relationships are historically conditioned and constantly changing. How does one, finally, "measure" social contradictions? So, both Soviet international relations scholars[10] and the neo-Marxists have dismissed Western social science, based on a positivist philosophy, as inappropriate for studying the problematics of either development *or* war and peace.

This leaves the Western social scientist in a considerable quandry. If he adopts a methodology that meets the standards of offical Marxist scholarship, that is, of the Soviet Union, he cannot avoid becoming a spokesman for Soviet foreign policy interests. If he joins the neo-Marxist club with its more relaxed methodological requirements and its genuine tolerance for full debate and scholarly exchange, he must develop not only the skills of dialectical analysis, but also those of the historian and linguist. While English international relations scholars are by training more at home with history, neither they nor the Americans are particularly proficient in foreign languages, some combination of French, Spanish, Italian, Portuguese, and German being important for undertaking high quality research in the neo-Marxist paradigm.

This latter problem is of course a rather technical barrier to synthesis, and perhaps less significant than those of world view and appropriate methodology. But it should be mentioned because some political scientists have "discovered" the neo-Marxist paradigm as an attractive arena for research, not fully understanding what may be involved if one wants to become a member of the club with high ranking. Without extensive training in history and language, the possibility of significant error increases dramatically. The odds are that the regional specialist rather than the international theorist has a better chance of making it.

Does this mean there are no opportunities for synthesis? Probably, if we mean by synthesis a melding of two paradigms rather than the takeover of one by the other. Yet, international politics and theory scholars should be interested in or at least familiar with the theories and research agendas of cognate fields. Such borrowing has, in fact, been typical of our discipline for a long time. The neo-Marxist paradigm in important and impressive ways outlines the sort of situation the typical developing country faces today, a situation that has received scant attention in the traditional literature with its great power, military security concerns. The development of the poor countries in some fashion or other is of vital moral, political, and intellectual concern, and the insight that their opportunities for autonomous growth are seriously limited by international structures is a healthy antidote to the conventional view that more domination from the center will provide the keys to economic success. We should remember, also, that the classical tradition of international theory has been based essentially on the European diplomatic experience, and may not be fully appropriate for studying even the old core questions in the context of Third World problems.

As we will elaborate in the concluding chapter, there are many valid reasons for acknowledging the importance of dependency and world capitalist-system theories. They have undoubtedly enhanced our appreciation of international relationships in both historical and geographical dimensions. But for the reasons argued above there can be no meaningful synthesis, a "superfield" of international theory, if the core concerns, units of analysis, key actors, and methodologies are different. Despite the relative diplomatic calm of the 1970s, there is no reason to believe that the vexing issues Rousseau, Kant, and the moderns have faced have been resolved either intellectually or in practice.[11] We may *add* to the agenda all those problems raised by the neo-Marxists if we can demonstrate that development problems are critically linked to the issues of war, peace, security, and order, but as yet there is little evidence to suggest that these core concerns can be illuminated in important ways by the present contributions of the neo-Marxist paradigm. (On the question of power, however, opportunities for collaboration, at least, do exist.) A healthy respect for the contributions of another field, and occasional borrowing from it, do not however constitute synthesis. For the time being, attempts to synthesize would probably have more the character of a takeover than of melding.[12]

Notes: Chapter 4

1 In the words of one of the foremost figures among the *dependencia* school, "many of the persons so cavalierly grouped together on the common turf of dependency ... could scarcely bear to sit together in the same conference room, so profound are the differences in their several ways of viewing current realities" (Cardoso 1977, 7).

2 See also the introductory essay by Rosenau and Hollist, and Hollist's conclusion, "Anticipating world system theory synthesis."

3 A brief discussion of the development of *dependencia* in Latin America is in Cardoso 1977, esp. pp. 6–7.

4 This is not just a matter of contemporary interest. According to Wallerstein, "the history of the world is one of a constant series of revolts against inequality—whether that of one people or nation vis-à-vis another or of one class within a geographic area against another" (1979, 49).

5 Wallerstein is equally open to criticism for his views of religion and culture which he portrays essentially as "rationalizations" for economic interests (1974, 48, 353).

6 From the perspective of American foreign policy, see McGowan and Walker 1981; Krasner 1978.

7 As, for example, the possibility of imperialism between developing countries. cf. Mazrui 1981.

8 Charles Reynolds (1981) presents an excellent analysis of various kinds of explanation in international relations, including case studies illuminating the extent to which economic, power, and ideological variables can satisfactorily account for imperialist policies.

9 Bull (1977, 288–96) provides interesting comments on the question of order and justice in the international system.

10 Among the grounds for dismissal are "rejection of the objective laws of history, disregard of the class basis of politics, attempts to study social phenomena using methods that are adequate only for natural sciences ... objectivist attempts to go beyond class and politics, [and] refusal to acknowledge the unity of theory and practice." See Kulbakova and Cruickshank 1980, 278, 177, for further Soviet critiques of the field.

11 F. H. Hinsley has argued, however, that in our generation we have seen a fundamental change in the international system "which will be even more different from the modern system than that system was for its precursors, and which will be so because its leading states will abstain from war with each other" (Hinsley 1981, 24).

12 Johan Galtung must be seen as a figure who fits into none of the categories employed in this chapter. He takes both a structuralist and actor-oriented perspective on international relations, and hence uniquely devises formulas for combining the peace and equality problematics. His work demonstrates both the possibilities and pitfalls of synthesis between paradigms. See especially his *The True Worlds: A Transnational Perspective* (1980).

5

Paradigms in International Theory: Hegemony or Pluralism?

The preceding chapters have outlined some essential characteristics of three different paradigms used to develop general statements and research agendas on international politics. All are equally concerned with theory in the sense that they offer cause–effect propositions to explain continuity, change, and system dynamics over time. They are not conerned with discrete events.

I have used the terms challenge, competition, and synthesis to suggest that some academics in the field of international theory no longer agree that the classical paradigm should offer the only, or even the paramount approach to organize teaching and research in the future. A perusal of academic journals, conference proceedings, newsletters, and books will readily indicate the existence of a significant debate. They also point to increased specialization in the field as some academics have, for example, begun to focus their research and theoretical activities exclusively on international economics, or developing agendas for alternative futures, leaving experts in strategic studies, general international politics, or decision-making to tend to their own gardens. To the extent that the neo-Marxist and global society paradigms successfully challenge the classical tradition, we can expect the field to become increasingly fragmented as each school develops its separate academic paraphernalia, including specialized journals, research institutes, conferences, newsletters, and the like.

The evidence of a vigorous debate is available to those who are professionally active. Another question is whether the challenging paradigms have had an effect on the level of teaching. This is a question of the transmission of knowledge and world views from one generation to the next; hence it is likely to have a greater long-run impact. A theoretical controversy confined to the pages of specialized journals or conference sessions is not often carried on outside the confines of academe. But a generation of students taught to look at the world in a particular way *is* likely to have an effect in many realms. Our assumption in reporting the research that follows is that textbooks are a better indicator of the "acceptability" of a paradigm than are specialized research communications.

Have the two challenging paradigms made inroads into the preserves of the classical tradition? Are scholars from other countries breaking the monopoly of theory "production" so long held by American, British, and other Engish-language scholars? The answers to these questions will come from a review of international relations textbooks in the United States, Great Britain, Canada, Australia, France, South Korea, India, and Japan.

Research Methods

One caveat is initially in order. The following report is not designed to be a worldwide survey of the field. No single author could do justice to such an undertaking, particularly in noting the various nuances in the development of the field and in reviewing what in some cases is an enormous literature in the indigenous language (Japanese or German, for example). The measurement of hegemony or diversity is a more circumscribed undertaking, one that can be done within the time and finances available for this project.

The countries listed are obviously not a representative sample of the field globally. We cannot infer from the results, therefore, any conclusions about trends elsewhere. But insofar as they include many of the areas where international theory as an organized academic activity has been taking place over the past few decades, we may end up with a fairly reasonable profile of the main centres of activity in the profession. I hope others will subsequently fill in some of the glaring gaps, such as Germany, Switzerland, Italy, and the countries of Latin America, Africa and the Middle East. Some additional confidence in the results is warranted when we call that international politics as a separate field of inquiry and instruction does not yet exist in many countries (Gareau 1981).

Finally, in discussing the "production" of studies in international politics and theory, we cannot expect to have completely proportional results—for example, if scholars in country A represent 5 percent of all international politics scholars in the world, we could not anticipate that they would produce 5 percent of all significant works in the field. Proportionality is unanticipated, in part because of the longer tradition in the anglophone countries, and also because of significant differences in scholarly opportunities in different countries. Academics in the industrial countries are by any measure privileged. They have available to them research funds, low teaching loads, sabbaticals, research assistance, travel funds to attend conferences, and libraries stocked with a vast array of books and journals. By contrast, scholars in many developing countries work under conditions that militate against quality research. Some hold two or three jobs. If they write, it is often for the mass audience at home, where they can earn a little extra money from newspaper or magazine articles (or sometimes for advancement in politics). Sabbaticals do not exist; neither do funds for research, travel, or library acquisition. In other words, the findings reported below imply nothing about human academic potential. They do say something, however, about the sociology of our profession.

For each country, we selected a sample—about one dozen—of textbooks in international relations in the postwar period. This presented no problems in the case of the United States, Great Britain, and several other countries. But for France, reasonable samples were unavailable. The low N thus prevents us from identifying trends over time, but some observations about hegemony and diversity can still be drawn. In the case of Korea, two general theoretical articles were added to the eight textbooks available to bring the sample to ten. For Great Britain, several books were included that may or may not have been written as textbooks (Burton and Bull), but they are widely assigned in undergraduate course readings and appear to have at least partly a pedagogical purpose. For India, several more specialized books were added to the meagre list of textbooks.

The procedure was to note (1) the nationality of the author and (2) the paradigm used in that author's work, for each book or article listed in the textbook's bibliography, "suggested reading," or reference section. For example, the first item in the "Selected Bibliography" section of Chapter 3 of my text, *International Politics: A Framework for Analysis* (4th ed., 1983) is Raymond Aron, *The Century of Total War* (1954). This item is then coded according to the nationality of the author (French) and the implicit or explicit paradigm employed in that publication (the classical paradigm). We repeated this operation for each chapter or, as the case may be, for the single bibliography at the end of each book. This resulted in a large universe of citations for each country. For the American-authored texts, for example, 4,002 references had to be classified. Obviously not each item was read; but the world society and neo-Marxist paradigm literatures are still young enough to be readily identified among the sea of works in the classical tradition.

The reference sections of textbooks are useful for this type of investigation because they represent the conscious choices of the authors. They are telling their readers—mostly students— the kinds of works they should consult for their own research and further reading. The references function as a barometer of the authors' general approach to the field, the works they esteem, and the other authors who they believe have made important contributions to the field. We assume that writers do not include in such sections works they believe to lie outside the field, studies that are unimportant, or items with which they are unfamiliar. Reference sections, "suggested readings" lists, and bibliographies may not be the perfect data source to inform our two questions, but they are probably the best readily available.

About 24 percent of the books reviewed did not include reference sections. In this case we reluctantly used footnotes instead. As the sole alternative, they provide a good survey of the kinds of sources an author uses to illustrate or substantiate his textual analysis; in some cases they also reflect authors' preferences for further reading. But one obvious shortcoming is that they do not necessarily indicate approval. An author might cite a major work in one of the paradigms only in an attempt to criticize it. Hence, while footnotes serve as one type of indicator of works employed by writers, no inferences about approval or disapproval can be made.

One final note on data sources. A few extensive textbooks, such as Georg Schwarzenberger's *Power Politics*, are mammoth both in the length of the text and in the bibliography listings at the end of each chapter. For reasons of parsimony, we omitted chapters that did not deal with central topics in the field. The omitted chapters are indicated in the tables.

Each reference was listed only once for each textbook. Second or further references to the same work were not counted; however, another work by the same author was included. We also excluded from the count all references to newspapers, government publications, and—admittedly a vague category having few explicit guidelines for judgment—obscure publications, including foundation reports, the publications of interest groups or other private bodies, mimeographed papers, and articles in journals unlikely to be available in a reasonable university library.

We used the criteria outlined in the preceding chapters in assigning the works to the paradigm categories. All items dealing with the actions and interactions of states and/or involved in the analysis of war/peace/security/order questions were placed in the classical paradigm (paradigm #1 in the following discussion). The behavior under review was of the diplomatic-strategic variety. This included the literature on international integration and, with the exception of Japan, most of the transnational relations literature if it was ultimately related to the diplomacy of states (e.g. Keohane and Nye 1977). Paradigm #2 (dependency theory, world capitalist society models) included works in which international relations are conceived *primarily* in terms of the exchange relationships carried on *primarily* by class actors, including economic organizations. Galtung's important essay on imperialism (1971) fits into this category, for example, even though the author is neither a Marxist, nor does he espouse the dialectic method in that article. The problematic is also important. Paradigm #3 (world/global society) includes the various studies published under the auspices of WOMP or its predecessors, works which elaborate models of a global society (Burton 1972), emphasize the global interest, and/or use individuals or issues as the actors or units of analysis.

The guidelines are not so strict as would be required in an elaborate scientific investigation. Numerous category judgments have to be made, and there is the possibility that one researcher's item placed in category #1 could, on some grounds or other, also find a home in paradigm #3. Given the large number of judgments and the overlapping or fuzziness in the three criteria, precision is impossible, and replication might produce somewhat different results. But we are satisfied with drawing a rough portrait, identifying general magnitudes and trends; more precise methodologies combined with large sums of research funds might produce differences of several percentage points, but the trends and magnitudes would be similar.

Finally, there is the problem of defining periods. For those countries with a long tradition and numerous examples of textbooks, the sample covers most of the postwar period. For other countries the time periods are necessarily shorter. For example, the first Korean-language international relations textbook appeared only in 1962. The lines demarcating time periods, where the N is sufficient to allow a dichotomization, are completely arbitrary. They represent nothing more than a line dividing the sample of textbooks into roughly equal sizes. They do not indicate any academic or theoretical cutting points, the case of Japan being an exception. For countries with a very small number of textbooks, such as France, we make no attempt to trace change over time. The titles and authors of the texts and other sources used for each of the countries apear in the Appendix.

The United States

Table A–1 (p. 150) lists the volumes reviewed for references to literature falling into the three paradigmatic categories. The sample of twelve textbooks represents about 30 percent of the general international relations texts authored by Americans for the 1948–81 period.[1] It is thus reasonably representative, meaning that the substitution of several volumes by others probably would not produce significantly different results.

A review of Table 5.1 indicates that the classical paradigm has been and largely continues to be the predominant organizing framework for international relations texts. For the entire sample, more than 94 percent of the references were to books and articles that explicitly or implicitly employed states and state systems models. In the United States since World War II, the classical tradition has held sway.

Dividing the sample into two periods, 1948–68 and 1970–81, creates a somewhat different impression. In the first period, the few references to paradigm #2 were primarily comments about Lenin's or Hobson's analyses of imperialism, but with no suggestion that these essays provide useful approaches to the field. References to paradigm #3 were primarily to world

Table 5.1 *Percent References to Paradigms #2 and #3, American Texts*

Authors: 1948–68	No. 2	No. 3	Combined
1. Morgenthau	1.3	2.5	3.8
2. Strausz-Hupé and Possony	0.7	2.1	2.8
3. Palmer and Perkins	0.6	2.0	2.6
4. Hill	—	—	—
5. Van Dyke	0.6	0.3	0.9
6. Organski	0.3	—	0.3
Average for Period:	0.6	1.2	1.7
Authors: since 1970			
7. Coplin	—	0.6	0.6
8. Sterling	4.8	11.6	16.4
9. Deutsch	6.3	3.5	9.8
10. Ray	8.4	5.3	13.7
11. Russett and Starr	5.6	5.4	11.0
12. Kegley and Wittkopf	1.0	6.3	7.3
Average for Period:	4.4	5.5	9.8
Average for Sample:	2.4	3.3	5.8

government schemes, again with no claims that these were relevant to the enduring problems of international politics. For the period, less than 2 percent of the references were to literature of this sort. The behavior described and analyzed in the textbooks was clearly of the diplomatic-strategic sort, in the context of the states system.

The works in the second period, in contrast, indicate a heightened interest in both paradigms #2 and #3. The percentages are not very high (with the exception of the Sterling volume), but they certainly represent an increase over the previous period. There is no discernible trend within the later period toward greater acceptance—perhaps another decade will reveal if there is one—but for the decade as a whole almost one in ten works cited in bibliographies and reference sections is to the two challengers of the classical paradigm. This may not be a sufficient number to suggest a breakdown of hegemony or a robust growth of diversity, but it does indicate, I believe, that the field as presented to undergraduate students has broadened to include the economic and underdeveloped nation dimensions, as well as to some normative concern about the necessity of developing a global community outlook to overcome some of the problems that continue to plague man.

Great Britain

Table A–2 (p. 151) lists the thirteen volumes reviewed for the study. This represents a very high proportion of all British-authored texts. The total number of references is much smaller than in the American sample, but should still be sufficient to provide clues as to the preferences and recommendations the authors have, or make, to their readers. The overall portrait is similar to that of the United States, but with even a more pronounced domination of the classical paradigm. For the period 1950–80, 97.2 percent of the references are to works in the traditional vein leaving only 2.8 percent to works representing the challenging paradigms. And if we remove John Burton's *World Society*, one of the early statements of the global society paradigm, the percentage shrinks to a minuscule 2 for the thirty years under review. The debate, to the extent that it exists in

Table 5.2   *Percent References to Paradigms #2 and #3, British Texts*

Authors: 1950–71	No. 2	No. 3	Combined
1. Schwarzenberger	0.02	0.05	0.07
2. Friedmann	—	—	—
3. Burton	—	1.3	1.3
4. Burton	1.6	1.6	3.2
5. Frankel	—	—	—
6. Northedge and Grieve	—	1.7	1.7
Average for Period:	0.3	0.8	1.0
Authors: 1972–80			
7. Burton	2.4	9.8	12.2
8. Frankel	—	—	—
9. C. Reynolds	2.5	—	2.5
10. Northedge	3.8	—	3.8
11. Bull	—	2.5	2.5
12. Frankel	—	—	—
13. P. A. Reynolds	—	9.0	9.0
Average for Period:	1.2	3.0	4.3
Average for Sample:	0.8	2.0	2.8

Great Britain, has hardly reached the level of undergraduate teaching.

Dividing the sample in 1971 produces only a slightly different impression. As with the United States, the early period was characterized by a sweeping consensus concerning the nature of the field and the appropriate subject matter for discussion. The references to works in paradigms #2 and #3 are barely even token acknowledgments of other perspectives. Since 1971 some of the works have moved toward a broader conception of the field, but there is certainly no visible trend over time within the period. The 4.3 percent references to both challenging paradigms is less than one-half the magnitude found in the United States for approximately the same period. This does not mean that British academics in international relations are unaware of the current debates, but only that they have consciously or implicitly failed to accord the challenging paradigms legitimacy or importance by recommending them as "further reading" to their students. The hegemony of the classical tradition is not under any threat in Great Britain.

Korea

In order to obtain a sample of ten works—the entire universe of Korean textbooks in the field—we had to include two articles in which only footnotes were available. But both articles center directly on key questions of international theory and so provide a reasonable indicator of the types of literature employed by Korean scholars. The sample is divided into two periods, one of ten years, and the other of 1976–82.

The portrait for the entire twenty-year period is one of extreme orthodoxy: 99 percent of the references are to works employing the classical paradigm. The figures for the other two are so low, indeed, that lack of knowledge of their existence, much less acknowledgment, might be a safe inference (we should recognize, however, that political conditions in Korea inhibit open references to Marxist and perhaps even to neo-Marxist literature). When the sample is divided into two periods, only a slightly different picture emerges: the rate of reference to paradigms #2 and #3 increases roughly sevenfold. But with a base figure for the first period so insignificant, this is not a dramatic increase. Korean scholars remain firmly committed to the classical paradigm. Only a few volumes make even

Table 5.3 *Percent References to Paradigms #2 and #3, Korean Texts*

Authors: 1962–72	No. 2	No. 3	Combined
1. Lee Yong-Hee	0.06	—	0.06
2. Choi Jong-Kie	—	0.9	0.9
3. Lee Kie-Won	—	—	—
4. Kim Hak-Joon	—	—	—
Average for Period:	*0.02*	*0.2*	*0.2*
Authors: 1976–82			
5. Cho Jae-Kwan	0.8	0.8	1.6
6. Kim Sang Joon	—	1.4	1.4
7. Rhee Sang-Woo	—	2.5	2.5
8. Kim Sang-Joon	—	—	—
9. Park Sang-Shik	2.1	1.4	3.5
10. Oh Kie-Pyung	—	—	—
Average for Period:	*0.5*	*1.0*	*1.5*
Average for Sample:	*0.3*	*0.7*	*1.0*

token acknowledgments toward other formulations. If Korean students are aware of current debates in the field, they must obtain their information from other sources.

India

Indian scholars have written few textbooks in international relations. In the list shown in Table A-4 (p. 153), only three volumes were written explicitly as texts. Yet international relations as an academic field has been established in India for several decades, and the output of books and articles on various facets of the field is extensive. In order to obtain a reasonable base of reference sources, we have relaxed the textbook rule and included nine items (the Appadorai book concerns general international relations but is not a text) that take as their point of reference the foreign policy problems of India. This may seem to violate the criterion on theory we used in the opening chapter. But most of these additional books are more than current affairs reporting. They rely extensively on the theoretical literature in the field, particularly that dealing with imperialism, as well as that favorite of Indian scholars, the theory and practice of non-alignment. Others bring in decision-making, conflict studies, and other areas of contemporary research. Hence, while we must approach the Indian sample with some caution, it does provide a rough indication of the use and non-use of the three paradigms.

The list covers an extensive period, although there is a ten-year hiatus between the first and second items. From 1958 on there is a steady stream of books. The gap between 1970 and 1975 serves as the cutting point for the periodization.

The references to paradigms #2 and #3 are significantly more profuse for the entire period than appears in Great Britain or Korea. Combined, they represent 9.9 percent of the total references. The figure is skewed, however, by the very large number of references to Marxist literature in the Sangha volume (item 1). If we remove it, the percentage drops to 6.4, which is still higher than any of the previous countries.

There is an interesting distinction between the two periods. In the first, numerous references to Marxist and neo-Marxist works appear. Even if we eliminate item 1, the resulting average for the

Table 5.4 *Percent References to Paradigms #2 and #3, Indian Books*

Authors: 1948–70	No. 2	No. 3	Combined
1. Sangha	52.2	—	52.2
2. Karunakaran	16.7	—	16.7
3. Gupta	3.9	—	3.9
4. Appadorai	1.8	1.8	3.6
5. Doctor	1.0	2.0	3.0
6. Rajan	11.1	—	11.1
7. Chakravarti	6.5	4.7	11.2
Average for Period:	13.3	1.2	14.5
Authors: 1975–80			
8. Kumar	—	3.1	3.1
9. Chawla	3.0	—	3.0
10. Rana	3.8	0.8	4.6
11. Misra, K. P.	8.7	—	8.7
12. Misra, P. K.	4.2	—	4.2
13. Singh	3.7	—	3.7
Average for Period:	3.9	0.7	4.6
Average for Sample:	9.0	1.0	9.9

other six works is 6.8 percent—also higher than in any of the previous countries. Yet this figure declines to 3.9 percent for the period 1975–80, a trend in contrast to that in other countries. We can draw no important inferences from this decline, except the obvious one that none of the neo-Marxist theoretical constructs has yet made a significant impact on Indian international relations scholarship. The acknowledgment of the Marxist tradition is more than token, but the paramountcy of the classical tradition appears under no threat. As for the world society paradigm, there is either sporadic knowledge of its existence, or a lack of regard for its usefulness. The nation state and the states system constitute both the core and the periphery of the field in India.

France

The number of books is regrettably low. Even today, there are only a few distinct undergraduate and graduate programmes in international relations in France, although numerous courses are offered in international law, organization, diplomatic history, and strategic studies. There are at least two journals devoted to the subject, but the most important one (*Affaires étrangères*) is oriented primarily to current problems rather than to theory. There are also numerous monographs in strategic studies and imperialism at levels somewhat more abstract than most journal articles but, as in the works of Pierre Jallé, they make no claim to contribute to a field called international relations.

Thus, the sample contains only three general books in the field, two of which were written explicitly as texts. But Aron's masterpiece constitutes such a significant contribution to international theory that it cannot be omitted merely because its intended audience is not a group of undergraduates. With the very small list, it is not possible to look for trends.

Table 5.5 *Percent References to Paradigms #2 and #3, French Texts*

Authors	No. 2	No. 3	Combined
1. Aron	3.8	1.0	4.8
2. Renouvin and Duroselle	1.7	—	1.7
3. Merle	13.5	0.8	14.3
Average for Sample:	6.3	0.6	6.9

The figures in Table 5.5 suggest more than a passing familiarity with paradigm #2, particularly in the volume by Marcel Merle. But the percentages overall are similar to those in Great Britain and thus strongly suggest the continued dominance of the classical tradition. The prevailing concern with diplomatic-strategic behavior places it at the core of the subject. The references to the global society paradigm are so few as to suggest that in France the Stoic-medieval-Kant tradition remains essentially outside the field. The issues raised in recent criticisms of the classical tradition have not been discussed in the French literature that is designed for students.

The Anglophone Peripheries: Canada[2] and Australia

Since the number of entries for these two countries separately is quite small, I have combined them into a single group, providing a total of eight books, most of which are in key areas of international theory, but not necessarily textbooks in the traditional sense. In combining the two countries, there is no implication that international relations scholarship in them is organically related. Indeed, it could be argued that Australian scholarship reflects English traditions and priorities (many Australians have been trained in and/or taught at British universities), while Canadian academics have had close ties with their American counterparts. Nevertheless, both countries have produced their share of works in international theory, as well as textbooks; and their inclusion in the study is important to help substantiate the point of the next chapter, namely, that the field is characterized by a national (or language) hegemony as well as a paradigmatic one.

The list of authors and texts is divided into two time periods with four entries each. As previously, this purely arbitrary division represents no theoretical or substantive watershed in the field.

Total percentage of references to paradigms #2 and #3 for both periods is seven, the highest among the English-speaking countries. There has also been a significant increase in references to the challenging paradigms over time; they have more than doubled since 1975. But the figures are skewed by the Pettman and Clark volumes. The former is explicitly concerned with the place of neo-Marxist approaches to international relations—a rarity among general books in the field—and the

Table 5.6 *Percent References to Paradigms #2 and #3, Australian and Canadian Texts*

Authors: 1968–75	No. 2	No. 3	Combined
1. Burns	—	—	—
2. Axline and Stegenga	—	8.8	8.8
3. Pentland	—	0.7	0.7
4. Pettman	2.7	4.5	7.2
Average for Period:	0.7	3.5	4.2
Authors: 1979–83			
5. Pettman	16.6	0.8	17.4
6. Clark	—	17.4	17.4
7. Miller	—	4.1	4.1
8. Holsti	0.4	—	0.4
Average for Period:	4.3	5.6	9.8
Average for Sample:	2.5	4.5	7.0

latter treats the Kantian tradition as one of several important modes for the reform of the international system. If we remove these two outliers from the sample, the figures for paradigms #2 (0.4 percent) and #3 (2.7 percent) are sufficiently small to indicate the continued hegemony of the classical tradition. However, for most of the books in the group, the figures reach a magnitude that suggests more than token acknowledgment of competing ways of characterizing the world of international relations.

Japan[3]

It was not until after the end of World War II that a rejuvenated academic interest in pursuing the study of international relations as a scholastic field independent of, but closely related to, other disciplines in the social sciences developed. As in the case of the early stages of the field in the United States, Great Britain, and Europe after World War I, agonizing war experiences were strongly involved.

One important change, if not transformation, has occurred in the process of international relations' development in Japan since the end of the war. While the study has been predominantly concerned with the problems of war and peace or systems and processes of interaction between nation states—the problematic and form of the classical paradigm—there has been a notable increase in the use of the dependency or neo-Marxist paradigm in recent years. Indeed, since the war there has been a virtual "school" of Japanese international relations scholarship which has adopted formal Marxist concepts, analytical devices, and world views.

But those books which are predominantly Marxist have been excluded from the list of selected textbooks on the grounds that unevenness of data can be expected unless the same ratio of Marxist textbooks was included in both periods (1950–8 and 1976–81) used in this study. Unevenness of data, if occurring in such a fashion, would be detrimental to the observation of a general trend in paradigm reference, particularly concerning the use of the *dependencia*/world capitalist-system paradigm. To the degree that such unevenness is avoided, exclusion of a whole "school" is justified. The reader should thus be aware that the sample is drawn only from the "mainstream" tradition of international relations inquiry. Yet no study of the field in Japan is complete without reference to the Marxist tradition; particularly in the early years of the field, in the 1950s, numerous textbooks with strong Marxist implications appeared.

Although samples have been selected both from the pre- and postbehavioral eras, readers should draw no inferences that changes in the latter period (1976–81) are dependent on or caused by the impact felt in Japan of behavioralism. This caveat is important because the hiatus between the two periods in the sample is eighteen years and analysis of books published during those years is omitted in the course of this investigation.

Since the rules employed here for the classification of citations and references in Japanese texts into any of the three paradigms may differ slightly from those applied in the analysis of the other countries, they should be accorded a brief explanation. All those articles and books which were not placed in paradigms #2 and #3 have been categorized as belonging to the classical tradition. Thus, paradigm #1 includes not only those items which employ the nation-state system as a conceptual framework for analysis of international relations (for example works by Bull and Hoffmann), but also writings which are not directly concerned with a system of states; these range from books on quantitative analysis to essays on political cybernetics. However, a strong case can be stated that political cybernetics possess, if applied properly, potential applicability to global modeling (cf. Deutsch

1977); with the central concept of communication applied to transactions across national borders. Nevertheless, the position taken here is that even if the applicability of a certain concept to all levels of analysis, be it individual, group, state, interstate, or global system, is fully recognized, this alone does not constitute a sufficient challenge to the classical paradigm.

Works on regional integration are also classified into paradigm #1. They are concerned with the process of nation states transferring their sovereignty to a higher organization, which may be no more than a nation state writ large, participating in the same old "power politics," but with renewed strength (Bull 1977, 265). This generalization is not meant to deny the importance of differences in approaches and the awareness of issues involved among different schools of regional integrationalists, nor to ignore their commonly held philosophical awareness (also shared by global functionalists) of the desired effects of peaceful change on international politics in terms of conflict resolution. In this respect, following the example set by Charles Pentland (1973) in the classification of schools of regional integration, federalists and functionalists are set aside from both neofunctionalists and pluralists, with only the latter two classified into paradigm #1 here. It is true that differences in methodology and emphasis exist between neofunctionalists and Deutschian pluralist-transnationalists; the former are more concerned with the final state of integration, whereas the latter examine the processes of change in social and economic conditions affecting political interactions between nation states. Thus it can be argued that if the methodology of the transnationalists is applied to the global system level, they could be more appropriately identified with paradigm #3. But, for the same reason as in the case of political cybernetics, the applicability of a methodology—more potential than actual—to all levels of analysis does not constitute grounds sufficient for placing the literature into the global society paradigm.

As in the previous sections of this chapter paradigm #2 includes the works of neo-Marxists (for example, Kautsky, Luxembourg, Bukharin, and Lenin), of *dependencia* writers (for example, Santos, Frank, Cardoso, Amin, Furtado, and Jaguaribe), and of the capitalist world-system writers (for example, Wallerstein, Chase-Dunn, Hopkins, and Bergesen). A basic assumption they share is that the structure and dynamics of international relations are the result of asymmetrical capital accumulation and conflictual class formation, both of which are the inevitable concomitant of the binary nature of the world economic system. Here again, however, two reasonable claims can be made against such categorization. First, not all the writers ignore or deny the line of causation from nation states to the world system. Kautsky's division of political imperialism from "ultraimperialism," and Furtado's or Jaguaribe's developmental strategy of strengthened national autonomy are the prime examples of this argument. Second, these works do not necessarily hypothesize uncritically that the conflictual nature of the world system is the political consequence of interactions only between the capitalist and the precapitalist, or of the developed and underdeveloped, systems. Some of the authors forcefully argue, also, that interactions between *state* organizations, which are competitive and mercantile in nature, cause severe conflicts, particularly within the multicentric capitalist system.

Although both of these claims do not disregard either the positive or negative functions of nation states, it should be emphasized that nation states, in the literature, are in the final analysis assumed to be one type of capitalist organization in the competitive process of capital accumulation and commodity production (Chase-Dunn 1979). This is precisely the dividing point between the discussions of world economies and hegemony, and of mercantilism, the former being characterized by the superiority of the economy over the state, and the latter by the opposite relationship.

The works that go into paradigm #3 are associated with WOMP and other world society theorists, such as Burton, Keohane, Mitrany, and Modelski. The writers categorized into paradigm #3 share the same ground in three dimensions: actors are multiple in nature, human activities of all kinds determine politics, and "harmony of interests," be it among nation states or between states and other actors, characterizes the ultimate nature of international relations. These three dimensions are mostly lacking in the other paradigms.[4]

Which of the paradigms has the highest rate of reference in the selected textbooks? The figures in Table 5.7 show that none of the volumes contains more than 30 percent of the references to works in both the challenging paradigms. The range is from 29.4 percent (Seki) to 2.8 percent (Hanai). Throughout both periods paradigm #1 has been predominant, but compared to other countries the rate of reference for paradigms #2 and #3 is exceptionally high.

Table 5.7 *Percent References to Paradigms #2 and #3, Japanese Texts*

Authors: 1950–8	No. 2	No. 3	Combined
1. Kamikawa	—	3.6	3.6
2. Uchiyama	—	10.6	10.6
3. Kawata	10.4	13.6	24.0
Average for Period:	*3.5*	*9.3*	*12.7*
Authors: 1976–81			
4. Mushakoji and Royama[a]	5.1	5.1	10.2
5. Mushakoji and Royama[b]	3.3	7.2	10.5
6. Hanai	1.4	1.4	2.8
7. Eto et al.	6.0	11.4	17.4
8. Seki	13.8	15.6	29.4
9. Matsumoto et al.	10.9	9.0	19.9
10. Tanaka	11.8	7.5	19.3
11. Saito	17.9	6.4	24.3
12. Hosoya et al.	6.5	13.0	19.5
Average for Period:	*8.5*	*8.5*	*17.0*
Average for Sample:	*7.3*	*8.7*	*16.0*

[a, b] Items 4 and 5 represent the textbooks *Kokusaiseiji-gaku* and *Kokusai-gaku* respectively.

The average percentage of references to works using paradigm #3 is slightly higher than that of paradigm #2, when the two periods are calculated together. But the average reference level of paradigm #2 in the more recent period has caught up with the level for the global society paradigm; the increase for dependency theory/world capitalist-system theory, and various neo-Marxist references, has been 5 percent between the two periods.

As seen in the samples here, there has been over time a slight increase in the references to the challenging paradigms. And in comparison to the figures for the other countries, the Japanese discipline has been on average consistently more diverse, even when, as in this research, we exclude all the textbooks which are explicitly Marxist. The classical tradition continues to predominate, but Japanese scholars cite the works of authors in the neo-Marxist and global society paradigms substantially more frequently than do their colleagues in other countries. Even though much of the transnational relations literature has been included in paradigm #3, in contrast to the other countries, the figures are not significantly inflated. Even before the appearance of this literature in the 1970s, Japanese textbooks made numerous citations—on average almost 10 percent in footnotes and bibliographies—to global society literature. Japanese students, we can conclude, have long been familiar with all three traditions in the study of international relations.

Conclusion

The data for the eight countries lead to one obvious conclusion: the continued paramountcy of the classical paradigm in the teaching of international politics. Japan is the single exception to this remark, and perhaps not a strong exception in any case. Even there, with its long tradition of diversity in the field, about 84 percent of the citations and recommended readings are, on average, within the classical tradition. The remaining 16 percent are divided fairly evenly between the two challengers. Because the number is neither extremely high nor increasing rapidly over time, we can observe no significant threat to the predominant position of the classical tradition. Still, from the point of view of diversity and varied themes in pedagogy, Japan stands alone.

For the other countries, there are two rough categories. France, Great Britain, and Korea are bastions of orthodoxy. The field of study remains narrowly conceived. While there is some obvious acquaintance with rival formulations, they are not considered to be significant enough to warrant inclusion in bibliographies or lists of suggested readings. The message seems to be that students are better advised to keep to works that are solidly within the tradition. There are a few exceptions, such as Burton's work, but they tend to be so few as to substantiate the generalization. They have not become the pathbreakers of a strong trend toward diversity.

American, Indian, and Australian-Canadian scholars sit between the Japanese and Anglo-French-Korean poles. While the figures for paradigms #2 and #3 are by no means large, they are generally in the direction of increasing magnitudes. There appears to be increased recognition of alternative paradigms; in many of the works reviewed, the field is presented in a manner substantially broader than was the case in the 1950s and 1960s. *Dependencia* theory, in particular, seems to inform textbook discussions of Third World states in international relations, and many others deal in one way or another with ideas emphasizing the notion of a global community, the interests of which are conceptually distinct from those of nation states. And many more have emphasized the importance of non-state actors, although none has yet taken the bold step to proclaim that diplomatic-strategic behavior as a subject of inquiry is completely passé. But acknowledging the more than token role of the two challenging paradigms does not mean that the traditional concerns of the field are being replaced. There may be additions at the theoretical peripheries, but as yet there is no synthesis or robust competition at the core.

Notes: Chapter 5

1 A list of texts and "general treatises" in the field is in La Barr and Singer 1976, 22–7. Our sample includes only textbooks.
2 At the time of writing, there were no Canadian-authored textbooks in French.
3 This section was prepared and written by Takahiro Yamada, Sophia University, Tokyo.
4 For the other countries in the study, citations to works by Morse, Keohane and Nye were placed in category #1 because they are ultimately concerned with the diplomatic behavior of governments, and with such traditional concerns as the nature of power and influence in international politics. The figures for references to category #3 in Japan may thus be slightly inflated. This does not appear to raise a serious problem of comparability because Japanese references to global society literature were already *marked before* the research on transnational relations appeared in print, mostly in the mid-1970s.

6

International Theory: An International Discipline?

> An advantage of the multinational examination of our discipline is the revelation that some of those cherished, parochial ideas ... accepted as gospel in one country have little relevance in another. (Gareau 1981, 788)

A model of an international community of scholars would include at least two related characteristics: (1) professional communication between researchers residing in different and separate political jurisdictions; and (2) a reasonably symmetrical pattern of "production" and "consumption" of theories, ideas, concepts, methods, and data between members of the community. There is mutual acknowledgment and acceptance of the results of inquiry. In contrast to an international scientific community, a discipline organized on hierarchical patterns of communication would be characterized by a few producers and many imitators and consumers, with knowledge flowing mostly downward from center(s) to peripheries.

Obviously no existing discipline, even in the natural sciences, approximates the ideal of profuse contacts, symmetrical production, and mutual acknowledgment. Scientific resources are not distributed around the world in random or egalitarian proportions. How inegalitarian they are is open to debate. But one fact is certain. None of the major fields in the theoretical physical sciences is dominated by the investigators of only two countries.[1] Hierarchy, however, seems to be a hallmark of international politics and theory. Most of the mutually acknowledged literature has been produced by scholars from only two of more than 155 countries: the United States and Great Britain. There is, in brief, a British-American intellectual condominium. The figures that follow will substantiate this claim. But in interpreting them, it is important to keep in mind the nature of the claim. It does not suggest that research and writing in the field occur only in two countries; rather, it is only that the work of scholars in these two countries becomes disseminated regularly *throughout the community*, while the works of scholars in other countries are acknowledged primarily in the writer's own country or geographical region. It is not so much asymmetry of production as of consumption.

But to argue that such a condominium has exemplified the field—that international theory as an academic profession falls far from the ideal model of an international scholarly community— does not tell us much about recent trends. The reason why the British and Americans dominated the field for so long may be quite simple: they did it not only through important intellectual achievements, but also by default. Prior to World War II, most other countries had no academic field entitled international relations, had little concern with its theoretical aspects, and offered no courses of instruction to students. As an organized discipline, the British-Americans had at least a half-century head start on the others. The reasons for the early development of the field in the two anglophone countries are numerous and need not detain us here. We can point out, however, that in cognate fields such as international law, diplomatic history, and international economics, such national paramountcy does not exist. The contributions of authors from a variety of countries have flowed for many years.

In recent years the field has developed in terms of courses, degrees, research institutes, and publications in many areas of the world. In some cases, such as Japan, there are also large national professional associations of international relations scholars. Enough time has passed since the days of British-American hegemony to look for evidence of the growth and maturation of an international discipline, and of robust indigenous development in other areas of the world. This chapter will search for evidence of increasing mutual acknowledgment and acceptance, for the decline of parochial information exchange patterns, and in general for movement in the direction toward the ideal model of an international community of scholars.

Some Methodological Considerations

To examine these problems, we have employed the same technique as in locating references to paradigms. For each volume, we identified the nationalities of authors cited in bibliographies, "suggested reading" sections, reference pages, and, where necessary, footnotes. We defined nationality in terms of the author's normal place of employment, not temporary residence, actual citizenship, or other criterion. The work lists John Burton, for example, as a British subject, even though at the time of writing his books in London, he might still have been an Australian citizen. We obviously could not collect personal biographies for over 10,000 total references in the project. Where there was some question about an author's nationality, the writer was placed in an "unknown nationality" category. In particular, there were some authors writing in disciplines other than international relations or political science who had anglophone names and even British or American publishers; we could not assume, however, that they were British or American, since Australians, Canadians, Irish, New Zealanders, and some South Africans commonly publish in the United States or Great Britain. The unknown nationality category includes 4.3 percent of all the references.

The work in some cases defines nationality in regional, not country, terms. We assigned to the European category all writers on the continent. This included Russians up to 1917 and East Europeans up to 1945. Marxist theorists were labeled Europeans up to 1917; after then, as communist. The Scandinavia category includes Icelanders, Norwegians, Swedes, Danes, and Finns. The other regional categories are those traditionally used elsewhere. The Middle East includes Israel, and Latin American includes the Caribbean, Central America, and Mexico. The northern African countries belong to the Middle East. The "other" category is residual.

There is a major problem in using references, bibliographies, and footnotes as indicators of mutual awareness and acknowledgment between authors of different nationalities. In the United States and Great Britain, in particular, where foreign language proficiency is of variable (and often low) level among students, a textbook writer might hesitate to list works in foreign languages on the assumption that students would not bother to consult them. There is no convention on the matter, but the fact remains that very few English-language texts include references to works in other languages. This already demonstrates a certain parochialism, because the books in other languages *as a matter of course* list works in nonindigenous languages. There is no easy solution to this problem. And because of it, inferences about trends toward parochialism or toward a genuine international community of scholars have to be made with certain caution.

The problem is somewhat less critical if we recall two facts. First, some anglophone texts *do* list foreign language entries (Schwarzenberger, Morgenthau, Strausz-Hupé/Possony). Second, many important works by nonanglophone authors are either written in English or are translated. Virtually all Indian scholarship is published in English, and Scandinavians frequently work in English as well. Overall, our figures for American and British references by anglophone authors are probably inflated because of some conscious decisions not to include the works of foreign authors in other languages.[2] In many other cases, however, the pattern of references is an accurate indicator of an author's reading habits, of his or her familiarity (or lack thereof) with foreign literatures. Even if we deducted 10 percent from the number of references to British and American authors, the overall picture would remain essentially the same. The general profile of our profession is one of highly asymmetrical communication flows between nations and regions. There is a British-American intellectual condominium in the sense that it is predominately the works of authors from those countries which disseminate throughout the entire community. Scholars from other countries "produce" a great deal of literature, but it is rarely acknowledged, much less recommended to students, by the textbook writers of England and the United States. Moreover, the centres of writing, of theoretical innovation, have many characteristics of parochialism and these are increasing. There are signs of diversity—witness the eager reception of dependency theory and the dramatic development of Japanese scholarship—but these have been as yet insufficient to alter the essentially hierarchical characteristics of international relations scholarship, as revealed in the literature directed to students.

The United States

In their reference sections and bibliographies, American authors overwhelmingly cite and recommend the works of their national colleagues. Even though the periodization is arbitrary, as one moves from the 1950s and 1960s to the last decade and one-half, an unmistakable trend toward *more* national concentration emerges. Five of the six textbooks written in the second period have more than 80 percent references to fellow Americans. Overall, there is more than 10 percentage points difference between the two periods. Removal of the two outliers, items 2 and 7, reduces the differences between the two periods by only 0.2 percent.

As the percentage of references to American authors has increased, references to British authors has decreased; the percentage for the second period, 7.2 percent on average, is less than one-half the comparative figure for the first period. These have been replaced by American authors, not by other foreigners. In terms of a British-American hegemony in the field, as indicated by reference patterns, there is no sign of a growing awareness or acknowledgment of the literature coming from

Table 6.1 *Percent References to American, British, and Own Nationality, American Authors*

Authors: 1948–68	Refs. to U.S. Authors	Refs. to Br. Authors	Refs. to Own	No. of Nationalities Cited
1. Morgenthau	62.4	20.8	62.4	7
2. Strausz-Hupé and Possony	49.1	15.8	49.1	7
3. Palmer and Perkins	67.4	21.6	67.4	7
4. Hill	75.2	10.7	75.2	8
5. Van Dyke	80.2	10.9	80.2	9
6. Organski	79.4	10.3	79.4	8
Average for Period:	68.9	15.0	68.9	7.5
Authors: since 1970				
7. Coplin	86.3	5.8	86.3	9
8. Sterling	59.9	17.0	59.9	9
9. Deutsch	82.1	2.8	82.1	11
10. Ray	80.0	7.5	80.0	10
11. Russett and Starr	82.4	5.3	82.4	8
12. Kegley and Wittkopf	84.8	5.0	84.8	10
Average for Period:	79.3	7.2	79.3	9.5
Average for Sample:	74.1	11.1	74.1	8.6

other countries. On the contrary, the combined British-American percentage (86.5) is higher in the second compared to the first period.

The only indicator of some increased attention to foreign publications is in the number of nationalities cited in each textbook. For the first period, the volumes examined cited on average 7.5 nationalities each; this figure rose to 9.5 in the second period. But given the strong tendency toward more references to works of fellow Americans, this increase means only that the larger number of nationalities has to share a decreasing pie of recognition. In sum, there is nothing in the figures in Table 6.1 to suggest increased American awareness of works by foreign authors; even the writings of British scholars, at one time a crucial source of ideas, concepts, and interpretations in the field, have declined to a relatively insignificant magnitude. As measured by references, American textbook writers have become almost totally self-reliant, a trend significantly at odds with the model of an international community of scholars.

Great Britain

From 1951 to 1971 British authors cited their compatriots and American authors with almost equal frequencies, suggesting the pattern of a British-American condominium in our field. Combined, these references on average accounted for more than three-quarters of the total. In the second period, the figures suggest more the profile of Great Britain as a scholarly little brother to the United States. British authors cite Americans with increasing frequency and their cohorts with slightly decreasing frequency. The difference in acknowledging Americans' work between the two periods is more than 13 percent. Since 1972, on average more than one-half of the references have been to American authors.

The decline in frequency of references to compatriots has not, however, been dramatic over the total thirty-year period—less than 5 percent. This suggests continued activity in the field. And since the large majority of references are to two countries, compared to the Americans' self-reliance, at least some intellectual pluralism exists. Nevertheless, the pattern is one of condominium, with more than 85 percent of the references taken up by the authors of only two countries. This leaves less than 12

Table 6.2 *Percent References to American, British, and Own Nationality, British Authors*

Authors: 1950–71	Refs. to U.S. Authors	Refs. to Br. Authors	Refs. to Own	No. of Nationalities Cited
1. Schwarzenberger	24.5	30.8	30.8	7
2. Friedmann	23.9	63.0	63.0	5
3. Burton	52.7	18.0	18.0	7
4. Burton	54.8	25.8	25.8	5
5. Frankel	42.3	46.0	46.0	4
6. Northedge and Grieve	42.1	31.4	31.4	6
Average for Period:	40.5	35.8	35.8	5.7
Authors: 1972–80				
7. Burton	60.9	26.8	26.8	3
8. Frankel	78.0	17.8	17.8	4
9. C. Reynolds	50.4	36.4	36.4	6
10. Northedge	41.0	41.0	41.0	8
11. Bull	26.8	40.0	40.0	9
12. Frankel	40.7	40.7	40.7	4
13. P. A. Reynolds	79.5	15.9	15.9	4
Average for Period:	53.9	31.2	31.2	5.4
Average for Sample:	47.5	33.4	33.4	5.5

percent (after deduction of the "unknown nationality" category) for all other nationalities combined—hardly the pattern of growing international awareness. The number of nationalities cited in an average textbook has also declined over the years, and is significantly lower than the comparable figure for the United States.

In sum, British textbooks, in their selection of suggested readings for students, can hardly be described in terms other than pronounced parochialism. The high degree of orthodoxy in terms of paradigm analysis is buttressed by a notable unacceptability or awareness of literature coming from countries other than Great Britain and the United States. And the trend is toward greater concentration, not diversity. Great Britain represents only somewhat less than the United States the polar extreme to the ideal model of an international community of scholars.

Korea

The pattern of references in the Korean literature shows a marked increase in references to American-authored works, and a corresponding—and quite dramatic—decrease in acknowledgment of literature from Great Britain. With more than three-quarters of all references in the second period to American authors, there is a profile which we might label intellectual dependency: Korean authors are overwhelmingly aware of, and recommend, the literature that comes from a single country, the United States, but American authors appear totally unaware of writings—even those in English—of Korean authors. Moreover, there is no evidence yet of a growing self-awareness. The percentage of references to Korean authors has actually declined slightly comparing the two periods.

As with the United States and Great Britain, the change in percentages over time suggests a trend toward increasing concentration toward a single nationality. This is not unexpected, because almost all of the Korean scholars of the younger generation have been trained in the United States where, as our data

Table 6.3 *Percent References to American, British, and Own Nationality, Korean Authors*

Authors: 1962–72	Refs. to U.S. Authors	Refs. to Br. Authors	Refs. to Own	No. of Nationalities Cited
1. Lee Yong-Hee	13.9	31.6	—	6
2. Choi Jong-Kie	56.5	20.0	2.8	8
3. Lee Kie-Won	70.6	—	11.8	3
4. Kim Hak-Joon	13.8	27.6	6.9	7
Average for Period:	*38.7*	*19.8*	*5.4*	*6.0*
Authors: 1976–82				
5. Cho Jae-Kwan	76.3	12.9	—	7
6. Kim Sang-Joon	71.2	5.5	2.7	5
7. Rhee Sang-Woo	75.0	5.0	10.0	4
8. Kim Sang-Joon	82.2	2.2	4.4	7
9. Park Sang-Shik	82.5	7.0	—	7
10. Oh Kie-Pyung	67.1	4.8	10.8	5
Average for Period:	*75.7*	*6.2*	*4.7*	*5.8*
Average for Sample:	*60.9*	*11.7*	*4.9*	*5.9*

suggest, there is little awareness of works by non-American scholars. Korea is the most orthodox country in terms of employing a single paradigm in scholarly work; its increasing reliance upon the United States for intellectual guidance is also in a direction opposite to diversity. Perhaps most distressing for those looking for indigenous development of a field is the lack of acknowledgment to the works of one's own countrymen. It is this dimension that separates Korea from Great Britain in the pattern of citations and references.[3]

India

In approaching the figures for India, we must recall that some of the volumes selected for the sample dealt specifically with problems of Indian foreign policy. We expect, then, that the figures for citations and references to works of fellow countrymen would be somewhat higher than in the case of the other countries, where only textbooks or theoretical treatises were employed. We can check this expectation by selecting out those Indian-authored books which are in fact texts or general works, namely, items 4, 5, 7, 8, and 10. The average citation percent to fellow Indians in these works is 22.1; this is significantly lower than the 31.4 percent for the entire sample. However, even the lower figure suggests a distribution fundamentally different than in Korea: Indians refer to each others' works regularly, if not profusely. Moreover, there is no trend toward increased reliance on American-authored works; the percentage has actually declined by slightly more than 3 percentage points when the two periods are compared. References to British authors have declined more perceptibly.

Compared to the three previous countries, India's pattern of references and citations shows considerably more diversity; less than one-half of the references in the second period are to British and American authors, combined, and the trend is toward continued decrease. This has been accompanied by increased references to the Indian literature, suggesting a certain amount of intellectual self-reliance. The number of nationalities refered to, on average, is also quite high (higher than Great Britain and Korea), although there is a slight decline from the first to the second period. The Indian pattern of references can be characterized as one of declining intellectual dependency, increased self-awareness, but not yet significant increases in

110

Table 6.4 *Percent References to American, British, and Own Nationality, Indian Authors*

Authors: 1948–70	Refs. to U.S. Authors	Refs. to Br. Authors	Refs. to Own	No. of Nationalities Cited
1. Sangha	43.5	24.5	10.9	6
2. Karunakaran	24.1	15.7	31.5	8
3. Gupta	31.6	9.2	48.7	7
4. Appadorai	20.5	16.1	51.8	8
5. Doctor	58.0	29.0	9.0	6
6. Rajan	27.8	22.2	33.3	5
7. Chakravarti	41.5	35.4	7.9	11
Average for Period:	*35.3*	*21.7*	*27.6*	*7.3*
Authors: 1975–80				
8. Kumar	64.8	25.4	1.6	6
9. Chawla	39.4	3.0	50.0	6
10. Rana	36.3	17.8	40.2	10
11. Misra, K. P.	24.6	26.1	28.3	7
12. Misra, P. K.	12.0	6.6	37.3	5
13. Singh	16.0	6.8	58.0	6
Average for Period:	*32.2*	*14.3*	*35.9*	*6.7*
Average for Sample:	*33.9*	*18.3*	*31.4*	*7.0*

acknowledgment of literatures outside of the British-American and South Asian contexts.

France

The lack of general works in French prevents the identification of any trends. With a very small sample of only three volumes, moreover, it is difficult to make any valid generalizations that could be expected to hold over time. The figures for the Aron, Renouvin and Duroselle, and Merle volumes at least suggest a pattern of considerably greater diversity than in the case of the United States, Great Britain, and Korea. References to the British-American community comprise about one-half of the total, but with a significant one-quarter of self-references. Moreover, the three countries combined account for only about 75 percent of all references, leaving another 18.3 percent (not

Table 6.5 *Percent References to American, British, and Own Nationality, French Authors*

Authors	Refs. to U.S. Authors	Refs. to Br. Authors	Refs. to Own	No. of Nationalities Cited
1. Aron	44.8	18.0	17.0	5
2. Renouvin and Duroselle	41.9	7.0	23.8	9
3. Merle	30.0	12.0	34.0	9
Average for Sample:	38.9	12.3	24.9	7.7

including the "unknown nationality" category) for other nationalities. Considering the extent of the British-American condominium over the field through the years, this profile suggests fair diversity, one that is more consistent with the model of an international community of scholars. References are dispersed among nationalities, there is considerable acknowledgment of the literature of one's own countrymen, and the percentage of references to only two centres of productivity is not nearly so overwhelming as is the case with some of the other countries. On a parochial-international dimension, the French reference data would tend toward the international pole, although there is much room for improvement as far as acknowledging and using works from the "peripheries" is concerned. France represents diversity within a Western intellectual core, much less parochial than the United States, but not yet cognizant of work going on in countries such as Australia, Japan, and India.

The Anglophone Peripheries: Canada and Australia

The profile of references for the anglophone peripheries contrasts in two ways from the other countries. First, there is over time a *diminishing* percentage of references to American-authored works, and second, a unique *increase* (mostly accounted for by Australian authors) in the percentage of references to British-authored works. The latter characteristic is skewed by the high percentage of citations to the British literature in J. D. B. Miller's *A World of States*. Yet if we select it out, the percentage of British-authored works for the second

Table 6.6 *Percent References to American, British, and Own Nationality, Canadian, Australian Authors*

Authors: 1968–75	Refs. to U.S. Authors	Refs. to Br. Authors	Refs. to Own	No. of Nationalities Cited
1. Burns	46.9	26.5	16.3	4
2. Axline and Stegenga	70.6	20.6	—	4
3. Pentland	64.2	16.3	1.1	5
4. Pettman	73.6	12.0	1.2	10
Average for Period:	*63.8*	*18.9*	*4.7*	*5.8*
Authors: 1979–83				
5. Pettman	38.4	16.1	2.0	11
6. Clark	47.9	28.9	1.7	7
7. Miller	37.0	45.2	4.1	6
8. Holsti	76.0	9.0	4.8	10
Average for Period:	*49.8*	*24.8*	*3.2*	*8.5*
Average for Sample:	*56.8*	*21.8*	*3.9*	*7.1*
Average for Canadian Authors:	*70.3*	*15.3*	*2.0*	*6.3*
Average for Australian Authors:	*48.8*	*25.7*	*5.1*	*7.6*

period is still 18, higher than for any country except Great Britain itself.

The pattern seems to be one of overall declining dependence on the British-American condominium, but without a marked increase in references to one's own countrymen, as in India; in fact over time there is a decline of slight proportions. The percentage of references to Canadians and Australians—national self-acknowledgment—is the lowest of any country in this study. There is certainly no hint of national parochialism. There are also indications of diversity: almost 20 percent of Australians' citations are to authors from other peripheries, and for both countries, citations outside the British-American condominium are more than 25 percent in the second period. The average number of nationalities listed in the references and bibliographies for the latter period is 8.5, second only to the American figure of 9.5. The overall pattern suggests heavy but declining reliance on the British-American condominium, greater awareness and acknowledgment of literatures in the peripheries (in this case, including Europe), but as yet no acknowledgment of an indigenous corps of writers who hold a position of approximately balance with the dominant nationalities.

Japan[4]

The mean values of the citation rates of American, British, and Japanese sources are presented in Table 6.7. From these data we can infer that for both periods Japan has been on average more or less self-sufficient, with its mean value of 43.6 percent marking the highest among all the nationalities except the United States. On the other hand, Japanese authors' citations to national colleagues is not sufficiently high that it could be appropriately interpreted as an indication of national parochialism. Rather, it is indicative of the Japanese scholarly community's openness and acceptance of the literature from certain other intellectual centres. Japan is followed by the United States, Great Britain, and Europe in descending order of reference. However, two warnings should be issued. First, references made to Japan and these Western nationalities constitute 95.5 percent of all references made in terms of the mean value for each nationality, leaving little room for other nationalities or regions. Second, the Western nationalities combined have the mean value of 51.9 percent, which is higher than Japan's value by 8.3 percent. Therefore, a qualification certainly needs to be added to Japan's independence and openness to foreign literatures. In other words, Japan's references have not been dependent upon any single national group of authors for the two periods combined, but they are highly dependent upon the British-American and European core. Japanese textbook writers have barely acknowledged or recommended the writings of authors from Australia–New Zealand, Canada, Scandinavia, the communist countries, and the Third World.

However, Japan's qualified independence and relative openness should not be considered a static condition. If the two different periods are compared, this point becomes more succinct. The data in Table 6.7 indicate that references made to Japanese authors in the more recent period not only mark the highest value of all the nationalities, but are also 3.4 times more frequent than those made in the earlier period. Therefore, we

Table 6.7 *Percent References to American, British, and Own Nationality, Japanese Authors*

Authors: 1950–8	Refs. to U.S. Authors	Refs. to Br. Authors	Refs. to Own	No. of Nationalities Cited
1. Kamikawa	21.1	8.3	10.7	5
2. Uchiyama	34.8	30.3	25.8	4
3. Kawata	44.0	24.8	9.6	8
Average for Period:	*33.3*	*21.1*	*15.4*	*5.7*
Authors: 1976–81				
4. Mushakoji and Royama	26.9	11.5	55.1	7
5. Mushakoji and Royama	40.0	3.3	51.1	7
6. Hanai	61.4	15.7	20.0	5
7. Eto et al.	51.5	11.4	32.6	6
8 Seki	26.6	6.4	57.8	7
9. Matsumoto et al.	9.7	7.3	78.2	7
10. Tanaka	11.8	3.2	76.3	8
11. Saito	10.7	8.6	64.3	6
12. Hosoya et al.	44.5	5.7	41.6	10
Average for Period:	*31.5*	*8.1*	*53.0*	*7.0*
Average for Sample:	*31.9*	*11.4*	*43.6*	*6.7*

can state that Japanese authors have increasingly acknowledged and accepted the growing field of international relations in their own country, and now accord it a status higher than that for any other country or group of countries. Japan's mean value in the more recent period is more than 11 percent higher than the aggregated means of Europe, the United States, and Great Britain.

This increased independence in references to indigenous sources constitutes a remarkable contrast to the high level of intellectual dependence witnessed in the earlier period. At that time, the rate of reference made to the Western cultural centres, including Europe, was about 5.2 times higher than that of references made to fellow Japanese authors. In other words, although Japanese students of international relations during the initiating stages of development were overwhelming consumers of foreign knowledge, theories, methods, and data, they successfully developed their own field and presently learn from each other's writings.

Table 6.7 also shows that while the reference level to American authors in the second period has remained at 95 percent of its level in the early years, in comparison Great Britain's level has decreased to only 38 percent of its previous reference level. The declining importance of Great Britain as a source of ideas, theories, and data follows the pattern of most of the other countries, but in a more pronounced manner. But this decline has been taken up mostly by incresed references to Japanese literature, not to "new" foreign sources of information.

To summarize, the analysis reveals that although during the early stages of the discipline in Japan the profile of references in textbooks is best described as a dependence upon the Western cultural centres, in more recent years the pattern has shown considerably more dispersion, with most of the change accruing to references of works by fellow Japanese authors. But while the pattern is neither concentrated nor parochial, the acknowledgment and use of sources from the Western peripheries, communist countries, and the Third World remains very low. Compared to the United States, Great Britain, and Korea, the figures for Japan suggest that Japanese authors cast their intellectual nets to a much greater variety of sources; they seem to be more aware that there is an international discipline in the field, major contributions to which are made by authors of various nationalities.

References in International Relations Textbooks: Toward an International Network of Scientific Communication?

There are several ways to measure degrees of concentration and dispersion in a set of data. Since the number of countries is quite small, and since within each country only a limited number of textbooks have been examined (although yielding a high number of references), we can employ simple descriptive statistics to demonstrate magnitudes and trends. Two related but separate questions guide the discussion: (1) to what extent is there a British-American hegemony, or condominium; is it strengthening or weakening in light of the development of international relations as a discipline in many other countries? and (2) does the pattern of references for each country indicate greater overall concentration or increased dispersion among many nationalities? For answers, we can compare and summarize the data presented in the first seven tables, omitting France in some cases due to the lack of observations over time.

The evidence provides two categories of countries regarding the question of a British-American condominium. In Korea, Great Britain, and the United States, the percentage of references to British and American writers combined has increased over the years, in the case of the first two countries quite dramatically. All of the increase, however, is accounted for by more numerous references to American authors; in all three countries, the percent references to British authors has declined. The experience of textbook writers in these three countries would indicate a pattern changing from condominium toward increased intellectual reliance on American literature; that is, toward monopoly.

For Canada-Australia, India, and Japan, the trend is toward lower reference frequency to British-American scholarly works in international relations. The decline of references to British authors (except Australia) has been precipitous, but in all three there has also been a decline—if considerably less notable—in percent references to American sources. The picture, then, is mixed. The authors of the British-American condominium are tending toward greater parochialism, while Korea's trend is toward almost absolute dependency on American scholarship. For the other three countries, increased dispersion and decreased dependency on British-American literatures seem to be the trend. As a group, the six countries show virtually no change between time periods; the concentration and dispersion trends

Table 6.8 *Change in Percent References to American and British Authors, Two Periods*

Country	Period 1	Period 2	Point Change	Percent Change
Korea	58.5	81.9	+23.4	40.0
Great Britain	76.3	85.1	+8.8	11.5
United States	83.9	86.5	+2.6	3.0
Canada-Australia	82.7	74.6	−8.1	−9.8
India	57.0	46.5	−10.5	−18.4
Japan	54.4	39.6	−14.8	−27.2
Average:	68.8	69.0	0.2	−0.9

117

almost perfectly balance each other. There is an average shift toward concentration of only 0.2 percentage points—not statistically significant—while the mean of average percent change shows a decline of only −0.9—also insignificant.

To answer the question regarding overall reference concentration, regardless of nationality, Table 6.9 lists the percentage of total references accounted for by the two most-cited nationalities. The most dramatic change has occurred in Japan, where a profile of substantially increased national reference concentration is evident. In the early period, references to the two top countries accounted for only 54.4 percent of all references, suggesting considerable dispersion of source reliance among several countries and regions. But for the 1976–81 period, almost 85 percent of all references were to Japanese and American works, leaving little for the remainder of the world. The figures clearly outline a case of increased concentration toward the authors of only two countries.

The profile for Korea is similar, if less dramatic. But there is an essential difference: the vast increase in concentration has been toward a single country, with declines toward all other nationalities, including fellow Korean authors. Such a high percentage of references to a single country is outdone only by the United States.

If bibliographies and reference sections are reasonable indicators of authors' acknowledgment and use of foreign literatures, then the figures in Table 6.9 for Great Britain have to be interpreted as outlining a situation of parochialism, combined with increased reliance upon the works of American authors. The

Table 6.9 *Percent References to Two Largest Nationalities, Two Periods Compared*

Country	Period 1	Period 2	Point Change	Percent Change
Japan	54.4	84.5	+30.1	+55.3
Korea	58.5	81.9	+23.4	+40.0
Great Britain	76.3	85.1	+8.8	+11.5
India	62.0	68.1	+5.2	+8.3
United States	83.9	86.5	+2.6	+3.0
Canada-Australia	82.7	74.6	−8.1	−9.7
Average:	*69.8*	*80.1*	*+10.3*	*+18.1*

trend toward increased concentration is notable. Great Britain represents the second furthest deviation from the model of an international community of scholars, of a genuine global network of communication, following only the United States. Apparently, British authors increasingly believe that little of scholarly note is being written in countries outside the British-American condominium.

India's pattern is also toward greater concentration. But compared to other countries, the percentage accounted for by the first two nationalities is much lower. Moreover, most of the growth has been accounted for by more frequent references to fellow Indian scholars, while there has been a decline in the percentages of references to British and American authors. As we will see below, finally (Table 6.13), Indian authors more than any other nationality cite the works of other Third World scholars; the pattern is actually one toward greater dispersion of sources if third- and fourth-ranked countries in India's sources are included.

The practice of American authors over more than thirty years indicates slightly higher concentration as measured by the first two source countries, but not of a sufficient magnitide to qualify as statistically significant. The change is only +2.6 percentage points (3 percent), almost all of which is accounted for by greater numbers of references to fellow Americans, and notable declines in percentages of references to the British partners in the condominium. No country approaches the United States in the percentage of references to national colleagues.

The artificial Canada-Australia group is the only category in which there has been a decline in concentration, using this measure. Most of the decline is accounted for by the Australian authors. The figure of −8.1 percentage points is not awesome (9.8 percent), but it is pointing in the direction demanded by the ideal model of an international community of scholars. Moreover, while the Canada-Australia category was the second most concentrated in the first period, following the United States, it dropped to fifth rank in the second period.

Taking the entire group of countries, excluding France, the trend during the postwar period has been toward more concentration of references in two top countries. During the 1970s and early 1980s, the percentage of references—in most cases to America and Great Britain—has increased over time by +10.3 percentage points, or a net average change of 18.1 percent in the direction of greater reliance on the two top countries. Today, the textbook writers in our countries typically recommend to their readers more than four out of five items from just two centres of scholarship. While they may well be familiar with research and publications emerging from other countries or regions, they are not acknowledging their existence to their readers. The British-American condominium is tending toward an American monopoly, but at least in Japan and India the vigorous development of nationally based disciplines tends to balance the large American preponderance.

We are unable from these data to say anything about "production" of knowledge in the various countries. What we can say, however, is that outside of the work of American and British scholars, very little else enters the international scholarly community network. Despite the impressive development of the field in India and Japan, the works of scholars from these countries are acknowledged and used almost exclusively in their own countries. This appears to be largely the case for all other nationalities and regions as well, although the percentage of references to European authors in most of our sample is still sufficiently large to constitute a qualification.

The general tendency away from an egalitarian model of an international community of scholars is modified only slightly by the figures in Table 6.10. These indicate that over time there has been an increase in the *number* of nationalities cited in the bibliographies of the average textbook. For the entire group, there has been an increase of 12.5 percent, or 0.9 percentage points. The largest gains in the direction of dispersion have been compiled by Canada-Australia, from 5.6 nationalities on average to 8.5, an increase of almost three nationalities per volume (51.7

Table 6.10 *Number of Nationalities of Authors Cited, on Average, Two Periods*

Country	Period 1	Period 2	Average
United States	7.5	9.5	8.6
Great Britain	5.7	5.4	5.5
Korea	6.0	5.8	5.9
India	7.3	6.7	7.0
France			7.7
Canada-Australia	5.6	8.5	7.1
Japan	5.7	7.0	6.7
Average for Period:	6.3	7.2	6.9

percent). The number of nationalities cited in the American-authored texts has also grown significantly, by 26.6 percent. Counterbalancing these gains in part are declining figures for Great Britain, Korea, and India.

But these trends—on the whole in the direction of dispersion—have to be compared to those data indicating greater concentration. The overall interpretation of the research is that while the work of a greater number of nationalities *is* being recognized, the *proportion of each, on average, is actually declining*. The percentage of references remaining after the first two countries' share has been used up is becoming smaller for most countries in the sample. For the second period, all other nationalities after the first two had only 19.9 percent of the total to share among themselves, while during the 1950s and 1960s they had 30.2 percent. Canada and Australia combined are the only countries which assign both larger numbers of nationalities *and* a larger percentage of the total references to them. Considering that these figures include an average of 4.3 percent authors in the "unknown nationality" category (but most in fact are anglophones), only 13.7 percent (France included) remains for what we have called the peripheries—including Europe.

Table 6.11 displays the distribution of the references, by country or region, to these peripheries. More than one-half of the total remaining references in this group goes to continental sources. The other Western industrialized countries—Canada, Australia, and the Scandinavian group—comprise another 25.3 percent, with all the communist nations combined holding only 10.2 percent. This leaves only 10.6 percent, including the "other nation" category, for the remainder of the world. Put in terms of the total universe of references for the study, this means that only 1.4 percent of the total is acknowledgment of works published by authors outside the Western industrial and communist groups.

Whether this is an accurate reflection of the distribution of international relations scholars around the world is uncertain. We would expect some rough relationship between the number of scholars in any given country or region, the number of works they produce, and the number that eventually find their way into the global communications network of international relations experts. But when the acknowledgment figures for the publications emerging from some countries, such as India, are so low, we could legitimately speculate that factors of parochialism systematically reduce mutual awareness and acceptance.

Table 6.11 Percent References to Authors from Peripheries

Countries or Regions Cited	Citing Countries								Ave.	Percent of Total
	U.S.	G.B.	Can.	Aus.	France	Japan	Korea	India		
Europe	5.2	6.3	5.6	6.5	11.8	8.6	10.0	1.9	7.0	54.7
Canada	1.3	1.6	2.0	1.4	0.4	0.9	1.2	0.8	1.2	9.4
Australia	0.3	1.0	0.2	5.0	—	0.3	0.7	1.1	1.1	8.6
Scandinavia	0.9	0.6	1.7	2.0	1.1	0.5	0.4	0.4	0.8	6.3
Communist	0.6	0.4	0.3	1.0	3.3	1.4	0.1	3.1	1.3	10.2
Latin America	0.4	0.1	0.2	0.6	—	0.1	—	0.2	0.2	1.6
Middle East	0.2	0.3	0.3	0.4	0.4	0.2	0.2	0.2	0.3	2.3
India	0.5	0.9	0.5	0.2	—	0.2	0.4	—b	0.4	3.1
Africa	0.1	0.2	—	0.3	0.8	0.2	—	0.3	0.2	1.6
Other	0.1	0.3	—	0.3	0.5	—	0.8	7.6	0.3	2.3
									(1.2)a	
Percent of Total Refs.:	9.6	11.7	10.8	17.6	18.3	12.3	13.8	15.6		
Unknown Nationality:	4.8	3.2	3.4	8.0	5.6	0.8	8.2	0.4	4.3	
Total (incl. all countries):	99.6	100.0	99.8	100.1	100.0	100.0	99.5	99.6		

a The Indian literature contains, in some volumes, a number of references to writings by Pakistanis, Sri Lankans, and Nepalese. The large number of "other" nationalities refers to them. The percentage in brackets (1.2) includes these references.
b Indian self-references (35.9%) are not included here because they would badly distort the averages.

Gareau (1981) has argued that quantitatively oriented American international relations scholars form a tight-knit "club" which has its own academic rules for membership, its own priorities for research agendas, and its own jargon—in short, a variety of devices which effectively keeps out those who do not share the mores of the club. This may be overstating the case in some ways, but there is probably more than a wisp of truth in the charge. The habits of scholarship are such that many academics confine their searches and reading to members of their own group—and often group boundaries correlate highly with national boundaries.

An equally important explanation for parochial influences that prevent literatures from entering the global communications grid is that many international relations scholars are heavily influenced by *national* diplomatic perspectives and priorities. While many academics in our field pride themselves as being concerned with international phenomena, they are in fact mostly involved in the investigation of those problems which litter the headlines of their national or local newspapers. Scandinavian scholars write a great deal about the security problems of their area; only a handful of Americans have even minimal qualification to discuss these matters. In the 1950s and 1960s Indian international relations specialists were no less concerned about the strategic importance of Bhutan and Sikkim than Americans are worried today about El Salvador. But few American academics—or any other nationality for that matter—have even the most rudimentary knowledge about the Himalayan countries. The authors of general essays and textbooks do not include references to studies of countries, regions, or problems that are not familiar to them. This form of parochialism must vastly reduce the search among foreign literatures. And even many works which have a high theoretical content, as in the case of some Indian writings on nonalignment, never enter the international scholarly network because the academics of other areas do not see nonalignment as a novel, interesting, or timely problem.

Whatever the explanation, the figures in Table 6.11 suggest a distribution of references that is highly skewed in the direction of the intellectual domination of traditional academic centres (United States and Great Britain), with very low percentages of citations accorded to scholars from the peripheries, whether in the West, the communist countries, or the Third World.

Table 6.12 ranks the countries in terms of the proportion of

Table 6.12 *Ranking of Countries, Percentage References to Authors from Peripheries*

Country	Percent Refs. to Peripheries	No. of Nationalities Cited
France	18.3	7
Australia	17.6	10
India	15.6	10
Korea	13.8	8
Japan	12.3	9
Great Britain	11.7	10
Canada	10.8	8
United States	9.6	10
Average for Sample:	*13.7*	9

total references given to all the publications of nations and regions in the peripheries, that is, to all the countries outside the United States and Great Britain, and self-references by Japanese and Indian scholars. Our three French authors rank first, although most of their citations go to fellow Europeans. None of the three books in the small sample had any references to works by Australians, Latin Americans, or Indians. The French also cited the lowest number of nationalities in their reference sections and footnotes. The bottom ranking is held by the United States, whose authors have at least the virtue of citing fellow academics from all regions of the peripheries. But overall, their figures reveal a marked parochialism, a pattern of communication that is highly self-reliant, acknowledging only British-authored works in any significant amount.

Australian authors rely most extensively on works published abroad. Its total percentage is only slightly lower than that of France, but the five volumes had, combined, references to all areas of the world. The percentages allotted to the Third World areas, small as they are, nevertheless exceed those of their American counterparts.

The final question to pose is whether this portrait of the distribution of references to the peripheries has changed over time. Table 6.13 presents the percentage point changes between the first and second periods. A word of caution is in order before we interpret the results. In many cases, the base figures are so small that a 100 percent increase or decrease may mean little. Trends are not discernible when only several citations are involved. For example, British references to works authored by

Table 6.13 *Percent Point Changes, First and Second Period, References to Peripheries*

Cited Country or Region	Citing Countries						
	U.S.	G.B.	Aus.-Can.	India	Korea	Japan	Ave.
Europe	-37.9	-5.9	-28.8	+0.8	-53.9	-65.3	-31.8
Canada	+20.4	+5.6	+11.1	-8.2	+31.5	+9.8	+11.7
Australia	-4.2	-0.1	-7.5	+11.7	+8.1	+4.7	+2.1
Scandinavia	+12.1	+1.1	-4.1	-3.5	+2.7	+9.2	+2.9
Communist	+3.9	+3.0	+9.0	-28.7	-0.9	+15.1	+0.3
Latin America	+6.3	+1.6	+3.9	-2.3	—	+5.0	+2.4
Middle East	+1.1	+2.3	+6.3	-0.1	-1.8	+6.7	+2.4
India	-3.7	-3.2	+5.7	—a	+10.8	+9.9	+3.9
Africa	+1.6	—	+5.1	-2.5	—	+4.2	+1.4
Other	—	-5.5	-0.6	+33.1	+3.6	—	+5.1

a Indan self-references (35.9%) are not included here because they would badly distort the averages.

Middle East writers increased from 0.9 percent of the periphery group in the first period, to 3.2 percent in the second. This is a large percentage increase, but in fact represents the difference between a single citation in the first period and two in the second—hardly an indicator of greater scholarly awareness of the literature from that area. Many of the percent point changes are of this sort of magnitude and therefore cannot represent any tendency toward one direction or another. Only three conclusions appear from the figures. First, there has been over time a steady decline in references to European-authored literature. The average percentage point change for the six countries, including Canada-Australia, but excluding France, is −31.8. Japanese and Korean authors in the second period have virtually ignored literature from the continent. This European "loss" has been distributed among all other nationalities or regions, with the largest portion (10 percentage points) going to Canadian sources, and the remainder divided among eight other nations, regions, or categories. Second, Indian references to works authored in communist countries declined significantly (−28.7 percentage points) between the two periods. This is not so much a trend, however, as an artifact of a single volume (item 1) which was largely a Marxist-oriented book. Finally, if it is impossible to discern trends of increasing citation to literatures in the Third World, by country, when taken as a group the signs are consistently in the direction of increased acknowledgment and awareness. But this increase has been at the expense of the Europeans, and not at that of the British-American condominium.

Conclusions

This survey contains some pitfalls, not the least of which is the assumptions we must make in employing bibliography, "suggested reading" sections, and footnotes as sources of data. There are dangers in arguing that scholars do not acknowledge, use, or admire foreign literatures simply because they do not cite or recommend them to their students. Few students, it could be argued, are sufficiently motivated in a field to read a book or article in a foreign language. Yet we cannot be deterred from analyzing the data provided by bibliographies because of these considerations. They may inflate figures (particularly in the case of Japan) but the general portrait of the inputs and consumption of knowledge into the international network is largely accurate. Some arguments supporting the research procedures have already been presented. The most telling, to reiterate, is that a large portion of the literatures in some countries and regions is usually published in English. The numbers of Indian, Japanese, Korean, Canadian, Australian, and Scandinavian scholars in international relations *is* large, certainly in comparison to the numbers in the communist countries and the rest of the Third World. Yet the figures in Tables 6.11, 6.12, and 6.13 indicate very little growth in the circulation of these scholars' works in the international network. Something other than language is involved.

The communications profile of the discipline that emerges from all the tables is one of extreme bifurcation between center (Great Britain and the United States) and the peripheries; increasing concentration; and for many countries, declining mutual acknowledgment. The overall trend appears to be flowing in the direction toward greater parochialism, away from the model of reasonably symmetrical communication among an international community of scholars. Balancing this picture to some extent is the strong growth of indigenous work in Japan and India, resulting in declining intellectual dependency. But there is no evidence that the works produced by Japanese and Indian scholars are reaching foreign audiences in any greater numbers than previously.

Perhaps we should not expect, say, English scholars to read works by foreign authors more than those of their cohorts. Most books are written for national, not international audiences. And as suggested, the policy problems—the questions that command diplomatic as well as scholarly attention—are not the same the world over. What excites the intellectual curiosity of Australian academics might be of little interest to French authors.

These caveats admitted, nevertheless the figures displayed in this chapter have a disturbing quality, for two reasons. First, at least the subfield of international theory is not supposed to have a national focus. The problems of a states system, the growth and decline of governing norms, the implications of interdependence, processes of integration, decision-making, and many other subjects that have formed the core of the field since the times of Hobbes, Grotius, and Rousseau, should be of interest to scholars no matter what their national roots. But the figures reported here suggest that international theory barely exists outside of the anglophone countries. If the vast majority of the work in international relations generally has predominantly a national orientation, then of course we cannot expect to see develop an actual community of scholars who share similar concerns. The field will have the characteristic of separate, nationality-based, international relations communities, joined feebly at the top in various international relations academic organizations, but developing independently of each other in mutual unawareness not to enhance global perspectives, but to promote national development.

Second, despite the vast increases in international communication, the larger number of international academic conferences attended by scholars from the world over, the proliferation of academic journals, and the growth of organizations which have among their purposes the fostering of greater international scholarly contacts, the pattern of the *use* of information for teaching purposes suggests great parochialism, and for some countries, a greater reliance solely on Americans to produce the new insights, theoretical formulations, paradigms, and data sets of our field. No comment here belittles those great contributions by American scholars, but one is inevitably bound to ask, given the information here, why the trends are operating in the direction of greater concentration when all efforts of scholars in their professional work is toward creating a community marked by genuine mutual acknowledgment and learning.

Notes: Chapter 6

1 This comment does not refer to applied research, where concentration in some fields is particularly pronounced.
2 Of the books reviewed for this project, only A. F. K. Organski's volume states specifically that the bibliography is limited to works "available in the English language." The problem of "inflation" of national sources is also evident in Japan.
3 Korean scholars write profusely about the problem of national division, and are certainly aware of each others' views on this matter. What is lacking is any mutual acknowledgment of works in general international relations or international theory.
4 This section was prepared and written by Takahiro Yamada, Sophia University, Tokyo.

7

Choosing Directions

> We first must establish what the important problems
> are and then make sure that the changes in the system
> really do affect them. To change the questions and then
> to conclude that models designed to answer other
> questions are outmoded is neither substantively nor
> theoretically sound. (Sullivan 1982, 212)

This essay has had two main purposes: to increase awareness of
the intellectual services various paradigms can offer to teachers
and researchers in international relations, and to enhance
mutual acknowledgment of scholarly work produced around
the world. The first objective is served neither by dogmatic
statements in defense of orthodoxy, nor by uncritical acceptance
of newer formulations. The second purpose is not advanced by
statements to the effect that the British-American domination of
the field is the result of some conspiracy, or that the rules of the
intellectual game are such as to exclude participation by various
national groups. For those who like neat, either-or conclusions,
the final comments in this chapter may appear undesirably
ambivalent. Yet the new debates about "realism" versus
"globalism" or about the merits of dependency theory indicate
that the substantive consensus in international theory has come
apart. The critics of the classical tradition have many telling
points to make, and all three paradigms make significant contributions *in their own domains*. The question, then, is not to
choose among them, but to decide which of them is most
appropriate for organizing teaching and research for *particular
sets of problems*. As the preceding chapters have sought to
emphasize, the selection of a problematic is prior to other considerations. And as Sullivan's quotation aptly puts it, it makes
no sense to criticize a paradigm for failing to enlighten us on
problems it was not designed to examine.[1]

129

The conclusion that the states system paradigm remains the most useful one for the field of international theory is thus not condemnation of the others, except where the others claim to take the place of the classical tradition, or where they lead to the study of trivia. It is the challengers' claims to *supremacy* or even equality in the field of international politics and theory that this essay rejects, primarily on the grounds that neither the global society nor dependency/world capitalist-system models is concerned essentially with the questions of war and peace, and secondarily because the underlying assumptions of the competing paradigms are incompatible. Their concerns with technologically inspired problems, exploitation, and equality— while eminently political subjects—are not the preoccupation of international relations scholars, whose concerns have been and remain those of war, peace, security, and order. No one has yet made a persuasive argument that the problematic of the classical tradition is no longer urgent or worthy of systematic study.

In evaluating an appropriate theoretical, teaching, and research stance toward the field, the scholar must be wary of two intellectual habits. First, particularly in North America, scholars are rewarded for innovation, and hence there is a built-in academic bias to search for new phenomena and new ways of looking at the international political world. Without strong historical background (of which North American international relations academics are generally short), there is an increased possibility of innovations being little more than old ideas rediscovered. Lack of clear originality is no grounds for rejecting ideas, of course, but authors should be circumspect in claiming novelty and they might also explore why those old ideas had not become an accepted part of the conventional wisdom. The idea of transnational relations, for example, was a major concern of many nineteenth- and early twentieth-century international thinkers. Their ideas did not flourish in the postwar era for the simple reason that all the liberal predictions about international contacts proved to be overly optimistic in light of two world wars and the cold war. Yet few of the modern apostles of a "new" paradigm which places nonstate actors and nonsecurity issues at the center of the intellectual stage seem to be familiar with their antecedents. Nor do they consistently acknowledge that their fascination with transnational phenomena stems not only from theoretical curiosity, but also from the same normative concerns that animated their nineteenth-century predecessors: the profusion of transnational contacts is implicitly or explicitly assumed to be a good thing, a trend leading toward integration, wealth maximization, and ultimately to peace, if new centers of loyalty can displace the worn-out nation states. Fewer yet have systematically explored the possibilities hypothesized by Rousseau, that such contacts are likely to increase, not ameliorate international conflict. This is only one example where claims to theoretical innovation are not entirely valid, and where examination of earlier formulations might reveal why they had been rejected in the past.

The second pitfall, which is related to the first, is the tendency of academics in our field to develop theoretical innovations on the basis of recent diplomatic developments—even before these developments have assumed the character of long-term trends or patterns of behavior. It is no accident that Rosenau's work, for example, was predicated on the decline of the cold war (e.g. 1980, 305) or that the general field of international political economy blossomed during an era of détente, commodity cartels, and demands for a restructuring of the world economy. The attractiveness of paradigms having core concerns other than peace, war, security, and order waxes and wanes with the course of international affairs. But a half-decade of enhanced harmony between the United States and the Soviet Union or a decade of world recession are not sufficient to justify the claim that the "realist" paradigm no longer fits with the facts of international life. A few agreements between Super Powers cannot destroy the logic of a system of international political fragmentation. Moreover, no "realist" of even the most pessimistic cast of mind ever claimed that international politics is *only* and persistently a war of all against all. Nothing in the classical tradition precludes periods of relative stability, the consideration of economic issues (as long as they impinge on core security concerns), or the inclusion of nonstate actors in analyses. Yet some of the more zealous critics of the "realist" paradigm have concluded that détente and the proliferation of nonstate actors are sufficient to establish the demise of the "old" international politics and its replacement by something new, even if that successor is not yet clearly understood.

International Politics: How Many Games?

Others who have pondered questions raised in the preceding chapters—primarily Stanley Hoffmann (1978, esp. pp. 106–45)

131

and Hedley Bull (1977, 50–1)—argue succinctly and persuasively that international politics today is an amalgam of many games, revealing simultaneously characteristics of pure power politics, collaboration, the effectiveness of international norms, the increasing importance of welfare-oriented issues on the international agenda, and even elements of transnational solidarity.

> Which of the models of international politics does the present system resemble? One thing is clear. The model of the [global] community is as irrelevant as it has been for more than four centuries. ... The highest allegiance of each actor remains either to himself or to a fragment of humankind—a bloc he belongs to out of necessity or conviction. We are still among the models of fragmentation, then. But which one? State of war or troubled peace? The originality of the postwar bipolar system is that it blended the two. The bipolar context seemed straight out of Thucydides ... while the restraints of economic interdependence developed in the other ones. The present is still a blend of the two ideal types. (Hoffmann 1978, 144–5; cf. Bull 1977, 41)

Though there are elements of all models coexisting in the structures and processes of international politics, it does not mean that a sensible approach to teaching and research must employ all of them in equal proportions (note that Hoffmann energetically rejects the formulations of the Stoic-Kantian-WOMP tradition). Choices have to be made—not only for reasons of parsimony—and priorities have to be established. What follows is basically an advocacy of the classical tradition, expanded but not superseded by newer elements of complexity, with war, peace, and order as the questions of highest priority.

The choice is based not solely on methodological or even factual criteria, for paradigms reflect value and normative positions. The attack on, and defense of, the states system paradigm is not only a question of isomorphism or theoretical scope. The debates which have been summarized in this volume have a largely hidden dimension of value preference. The problem of emphasizing a particular approach to the field is thus more complex than is implied in the argument that each paradigm views a single reality from a different perspective. The real difficulty, as suggested in Chapter 4, is that the value premises of the paradigms are often incompatible.

First, between *dependencia* theorists and those who have outlined some of the essential characteristics of interdependence, that is, the global society models, there is the philosophical incompatibility about *autonomy*. Dependency writers criticize multinational corporations and all forms of capitalist "penetration" because in addition to exploiting, they violate the autonomy of the developing countries—that is, they deny effective control over the essential decisions affecting a developing country's economy (strangely, these same writers ignore the foreign activities of socialist state trading companies). A dimension of the dependency problematic is thus national autonomy, as well as development. But all the statements from theorists of interdependence imply that enhanced autonomy is impossible or improbable—and probably undesirable—in a world characterized by the inevitable interpenetration of societies. There is thus a fundamental normative incompatibility between a school of thought which generally sees progressive and life-enhancing possibilities emanating from the technological and communications web that draws political communities ever closer to each other; and another school which characterizes those trends as inherently exploitative and autonomy-stifling. While from a policy perspective, perhaps there is a mixture of policies that could establish some balance between the desire for autonomy and the imperatives of technological modernization, the writings of most theorists in the two schools of thought are not reconcilable.

Second, global society formulations and dependency theories disagree fundamentally on long-range goals. Dependency theory posits capitalism as the mechanism of exploitation on a world scale, while the WOMP formulations of a problematic do not attach man's present predicament to any particular economic order. The genesis of global problems lies in *any* economic activity undertaken at the national level without regard to the global repercussions (Scott 1982). The normative position of many global modelers is to modify man's wants, to make them more consistent with available and future resources. But most dependency theorists argue that there can be no equality until every society has reached the economic levels of the industrial West (though with a socialist economy) (Holsti 1975). The goals are industrialism, urbanism, technological sophistication and innovation, mass culture, and the like—all of which are rejected by WOMPists as incompatible with the globe's carrying capacity. Ecological disaster will have engulfed mankind long before 160-odd countries enjoy living standards on par with those of the leading industrial countries today.

A third contradiction, regarding possibilities of fundamental social change, is between the global society thinkers on the one hand, and writers who carry on in the Rousseauian version of the classical tradition. The former identify various trends as progressive, leading eventually to a transcendence of the states system. Acknowledging few of the Grotian characteristics of international society, they proclaim a superior normative teleology to the processes they investigate, whether international class solidarity or the development of a world culture. The emergence of a uniform world culture is already a reality, and a transformation in human consciousness is occurring that will someday provide escape from the irrational struggle for national advantage. Writers from Thucydides to Morgenthau and beyond, on the other hand, see little but recurrence, patterns, and international politics characterized as a struggle for peace, domination, security, and occasionally order— regardless of underlying technological or cultural trends. There may be a periodicity to wars and peace, and the rates of war involvement by major and minor powers may vary considerably. But in essence, the study of international politics is the study of a game whose *essential characteristics cannot be transcended* solely by technological innovations (nuclear weapons being a possible exception) or a shrinking world.

Fourth, global society models are inconsistent with the states system paradigm along several other dimensions. The former include the idea of a "global interest," an identifiable consensus that exists distinct from, and inconsistent with, national interests. The latter denies such an interest. The only "global" interest of the states system is the survival of the system itself— for which many devastating wars have been fought in the last two hundred years. The fact of political fragmentation, as Hoffmann reminds us, has not been overcome by proclamations of mankind's unity, much less by technology or the expanded travel horizons of the average tourist. The evidence of a notion of international security remains scant, whatever the prescriptions of the United Nations Charter. Every effort to create a viable collective security organization—a moderate step toward a genuine political world community—has foundered against the rocks of political-military fragmentation. The reasons for Rousseau's rejection of his own perpetual peace plan, along with Saint-Pierre's, are no less relevant today than they were in the late eighteenth century. The merits of the global society models (see below) are not to be overlooked, but in general it is difficult to disagree with Martin Wight's conclusion (1966b, 27): "In progressivist international theories, the conviction usually precedes the evidence. . . . And when the conviction is analyzed or disintegrates, one is apt to find at the centre of it what might be called the argument from desperation."

Finally, there is the incompatibility between all three paradigms regarding the ultimate fate of the states system. Dependency and global society theories point in the direction of transcendence, or at a minimum, deep structural change. Their rejection of the states system paradigm is not based solely on its theoretical or empirical inadequacies. In addition, there is the bitter disappointment that the system has not "performed" better. Wars continue, governments cannot collaborate to ameliorate global problems, and world capitalism continues to exploit the poor and the weak. This is a system that cries for structural reform as a minimum, and replacement as a maximum.

Advocates of the states system paradigm as the preferred theoretical platform for the study of international politics may display their value concerns less distinctly, but they are there nevertheless. These include, as suggested, the value of political pluralism and diversity, particularly when contrasted to the alternatives of a "global socialist society," a world government, or a global empire run either by commissars or technocrats. Whatever the fratricidal strife resulting from political fragmentation, the historical experience of empires has hardly been one of stability and harmony. The states system does have important elements of order (including nuclear weapons), and periods of relative peace and collaboration. War remains the endemic problem, but given the choice between the uncertain probabilities of war and the certain necessity of oppression in any system that transcends the states system, it is better to keep what we have got.

This list of incompatibilities and contradictions, as well as those introduced in Chapter 4, is by no means exhaustive, but it should be sufficient to illustrate the deep normative and value cleavages that exist between them, and thus the barriers to synthesis. The incompatibilities are, however, not only in the realm of values. Empirical shortcomings are also important. What are the telling points that the critics of the classical tradition make? In what ways are the more than 90 percent of the works cited in the textbook literature insufficient? What is the matter with paradigmatic orthodoxy?

The Critique of the States System Paradigm

I believe the works of the critics are adequately known so that they do not need extensive recapitulation here. Were we to analyze every single criticism, moreover, we would delve into detail not necessary for a general analysis such as this. In any event, Michael Sullivan has prepared a useful summary of the literature, as well as an evaluation of the empirical evidence regarding the debate (Sullivan 1982, esp. pp. 197–216). The critics' main points are:

1 In light of the rise of welfare goals in most societies, the role and functions of the state have changed dramatically, and nonstate actors have become important in international processes.
2 The international diplomatic agenda is no longer limited, as it was in the states system era, to territorial/security questions. It now concerns a much broader range of issues. Outcomes in international conflict no longer depend upon the behavior of diplomats and generals, but also on the activities of businessmen, scientists, technicians, and a host of other players. Power—the ability to determine agendas and outcomes—no longer depends on military capabilities.
3 There are unprecedented levels of interdependence which vastly increase vulnerabilities and interpenetration, and which break down the distinction between domestic and foreign policies. The model of billiard balls aligning and realigning and sometimes warring is a totally deficient metaphor for the complex world of today.
4 With the development of nuclear weapons, war is no longer a major option. Among the major powers, it is not the politics of war and defense, but the politics of deterrence.
5 And, finally, "both sectoral and structural studies of international political economy clearly demonstrate the failings of state centric analyses" (Tooze 1981, 134).

This is an impressive (though not exhaustive) array of criticisms, certainly profound enough to indicate that mere repetition of studies along well-worn paths may not do for the future. The question is not whether adjustments are necessary—clearly they are—but whether new paradigms are necessary. This is Rosenau's question: shall we just meddle or

136

muddle with the states system paradigm, or shall we start from scratch on the assumption that the old model or any of its versions is *essentially* faulty? Before that question can be answered, the countercriticisms enunciated by Bull, Northedge, Sullivan, and others have to be outlined as well. I will add a few thoughts of my own to the summary.

(1) Nonstate actors are neither new phenomena in international politics, nor, despite their recent profusion, do they vitally affect questions of war, peace, security, and order. What were the Fuggers, Rothschilds, anti-slavery societies, pirates, giant cartels, and the Catholic church, if not nonstate actors deeply involved in the domestic political questions of many countries? All of these and many others played significant roles in the low and high politics, domestic and diplomatic, of the traditional states system. Even if more recently they have proliferated at unprecedented rates, there is no systematic evidence to suggest that they have any determining role in the generation, handling, or solution of international problems relating to war and peace. A few exceptions, like the PLO, prove the rule. They should not be used to indicate universal trends.

(2) The PLO is a poor example in any case because its objective is to become an actor like all other states. This is true for all national liberation movements. Cornelia Navari (1978, 121) has made a useful distinction between agents and actors. The two should not be equated. The notion of sovereignty was developed just for the reason of separating the two. There can be all sorts of international or transnational actors, but only states are legitimate agents of the system. A few would-be agents, such as the PLO, may be granted special privileges consistent with statehood (observer status in the United Nations) but we have yet to see the day when other types of actors are allowed entry into the club. Nonstate actors may well influence the course of international politics, but ultimate decisions on war, peace, security, and order depend solely upon the public authorities of states, made in the name of states.

(3) If nonstate actors are not new as transnational phenomena, then how could we ever decide what level of profusion they must reach before we have a new type of international politics? At what point do transnational relations alter the fundamental logic of political fragmentation? How many MNCs, INGOs, IGOs, and individuals acting across state boundaries for their separate purposes must there be to render the states system model genuinely obsolete? The mere existence

137

of a phenomenon, no matter in what quantity, is insufficient reason to accept its theoretical importance. To qualify for inclusion, much less to justify entirely new models, the new phenomena must demonstrably and crucially affect either the states system's *structures* or the *essential* processes, or preferably both, in such a manner that a new *kind* of politics is evident. Of the many critiques of the classical paradigm, only Keohane and Nye's *Power and Interdependence* successfully captures the consequences of new phenomena in international relations. But in selecting only nonsecurity issue areas to examine, they loaded the dice in favour of a "complex interdependence" model; they did not render the old model obsolete in terms of what it was designed to illuminate—the causes of war and the conditions of peace. This work and its predecessor volume on transnational organizations added to the field but did not challenge the core importance of the states system paradigm for games that are relevant to it.

(4) If there has been a proliferation of nonstate actors in recent years, there has also been a proliferation of states—almost quadrupling in less than forty years. This phenomenal development must lead us to be suspicious about the claim that the state-centric paradigm is obsolete (cf. Holsti 1980a, 52–4). Indeed, the argument that national boundaries are increasingly irrelevant, that governments can no longer fulfill their traditional functions, or that man must learn to think in global-centric ways must sound strange to those who have finally achieved the objective of countless national liberation movements: national independence. Government structures of many new states may be porous, corrupt, inefficient, and display many other indicators of conditional viability; but leaders consistently strive to create stronger structures to control transnational processes. They are not collapsing in the face of some modern technological or interdependence imperative. The thrust of domestic policies is in the direction of giving economic, political, and cultural meaning to formal sovereignty, not toward accommodation with either nonstate actors or with the realities of a shrinking world. It seems peculiar, moreover, that while many Western academics applaud every manifestation of national independence in Southern Africa or Eastern Europe, they simultaneously decry the continued existence, abstractly, of the nation state.

(5) The numerous empirical studies that have examined transnational phenomena and the role of nonstate actors, as

suggested above and discussed in detail in Sullivan's work, demonstrate only *activity*, including agenda-formation, but not *influence* on the critical issues of international politics. If researchers want to discover that some bureau of a government department runs its own "foreign policy," this should not astonish anyone who has studied the field. But ask what the scope and importance of an issue is, and the answer will invariably be that the key decisions relating to war, peace, security, order, arms control, and the like are not made by such administrative units. That they may influence the final choices goes without saying; but by themselves they do not make authoritative decisions or have the final word on these issues. Bureaucratic politics are essentially concerned with policy implementation rather than initiation. A variety of studies, including Nye's (1976) examination of the Canadian-American relationship that is particularly profuse with nonstate actors and transnational relationships, underscore the extent to which conflicts ultimately go to the top levels of government if sufficiently important stakes are involved.[2] The qualifier is all important. Numerous other studies chronicle the victory of "state" preferences when these conflict with the policies and interests of nonstate actors.

If a researcher wants to study the coordination of labor policies among Scandinavian states, or trucking regulations between Canada and the United States, or research funding for agriculture in the EEC, the activities of thousands of nonstate groups will become abundantly visible. But at a certain point readers' attention may wane as the magnitude of the issues reaches the peripheries of triviadom. Some are likely to ask, who cares? The classical paradigm provides a problematic that has guided research and theoretical speculation for more than three hundred years; it has not been rendered less critical or less theoretically interesting just because we can now prove that some groups carry on activities across national borders and occasionally carry a little clout that spills over into the diplomatic arena.

In sum, as Hoffmann has queried (1978, 109, 112, 161), adding actors and complexity may affect the varieties of behavior observed, but do they transform the logic of international politics? Does the addition of nonstate actors and transnational processes make such a difference that new models are required? None of the critics of the state-centric paradigm has effectively demonstrated how the crucial consequences of diffuse and fragmented power and the lack of a central authority have fundamentally changed. New types of actors, a shrinking world, international demonstration effect, multinational corporations, and a plethora of other phenomena which supposedly justify the obsolescence of the state-centric paradigm in fact loom important *only when the problematic is changed*. Perhaps under those circumstances, we need new models—but they would not be models of international politics.

The Contributions of the Challengers

Thus, in evaluating paradigms and the vast literatures they have spawned, the theorist and researcher must keep at the forefront of thought the nature of the problem and why it is worth studying. Sullivan's comment which opens this chapter is essential to recall when the issues are debated. To investigate phenomena just because they are there will lead to mindless empiricism, to a stretching of the boundaries of the field beyond anyone's capacity to see the forest instead of trees or groves of trees. Fragmentation, overspecialization, and a loss of normative concerns are academic consequences of a field which has lost its bearings, its fundamental purpose. And in terms of international theory, general propositions, broad understanding across time and space, and recurrence would give way to micro theory, to statements couched in terms of specific actors at specific times on specific issues.

Obviously the traditional paradigm has to be expanded to account for and measure the influence of new types of core objectives of states. Many have noted recently that traditional power-territorial issues have been supplemented by welfare goals. The tableau of essential services which states must provide has been broadened to include many economic stakes and technological issues—in general those kinds of concerns that have animated the redevelopment of international political economy as a field of inquiry.

There is nothing in the classical paradigm which prevents this sort of shift or broadening. Already many have urged that the concept of national security has to be reexamined in light of new types of vulnerabilities. Threats of the kind faced by weak new states that depend on the export of a small range of commodities may be no less compelling in terms of national viability than the older types of military threats, for example. If the classical paradigm could survive a shift of state core interests and objectives from those of the dynastic type in the eighteenth century to ethnic unity, national independence, colonial expansion, and the like in the nineteenth and early twentieth centuries, why should it be unable to adapt to new types of values and stakes today? Traditional "security politics" can include or exclude economic and other dimensions. Indeed, the classical paradigm *has* to accommodate itself to the particular concerns of many developing countries, concerns that for the most part did not exist at the time Grotius, Hobbes, and Rousseau were writing. How exactly this should be done—whether by studying autonomy and vulnerability-reducing techniques, the possibilities of collective self-reliance, or the impact of global economic structures on local decision-making—is beyond the scope of this discussion.[3] Dependency theory has important insights that can be employed in terms of the traditional problematic broadly conceived; but this does not imply that the researcher/theorist has to adopt the dependency world view in toto.

Global modelists face many problems of acceptance, but they have made powerful cases to the effect that problems other than war, peace, security, and order require systematic attention. Scott (1982) has demonstrated that important theoretical formulations accounting for the genesis of these problems are possible. But how the problems are ultimately handled will depend upon political processes and bargaining within the context of the nation-state system. The logic of the stag hunt does not disappear just because the nature of the problem changes or because the agenda expands. Whatever may be desirable in the way of developing some concepts of a global interest, governments will continue to organize their policies in terms of reasonably short-term calculations reflecting the configuration of power and influence in domestic societies, as well as international pressures. Whatever politicians' platitudes about world peace, global economic recovery, the fight against pollution, the world food problem, or population, their decisions ultimately are designed to enhance national priorities. If those happen to coincide with some crude notion of a global interest, so much the better. To condemn the nation-state system because its constituent units generally fail to abide by notions of global interest may be satisfying from a normative point of view, but it does little to enhance international theory as a discipline with scientific pretensions.

Ultimately, the focus we give to the field, in teaching and research, will reflect our own personal interests; and no one yet has satisfactorily explained why person A is interested in phenomenon x, while person B wants to devote his or her intellectual talents to studying y or z. But it would help if each were clear exactly why any course of inquiry is important. An international relations scholar who studies world pollution problems is explicitly or implicitly stating that these require more attention than the traditional problems; or, he or she can make the claim that somehow our understanding of the traditional problematic is enhanced by studying pollution problems. But without an explicit theoretical frame of reference, there is the risk of studying something just because it is there.

Global modelists have also criticized the state-centric tradition for its view of perpetual war and rivalry between states. But as already suggested throughout previous chapters, only the Rousseauian model of international politics is excessively pessimistic. The classical tradition, as integration studies have demonstrated, can accommodate peaceful relations and does acknowledge the possibility of common objectives. Even Morgenthau, who is most often criticized for his pessimism, acknowledged as early as 1939 the existence of common interests, the great range of possibilities for international collaboration, and peaceful stages in international history. Like Hobbes, he has often been misunderstood on this. The point he was making is that there is no "community" which generates norms and law *independently of the actors in the community*. To claim that states are guided by self-interest does not lead to the conclusion that their relations lead only to power struggles and war (Amstrop 1978).

Our survey demonstrates that the vast majority of studies cited in international relations texts explicitly or implicitly employ the classical paradigm and equate "security politics" with the core of the field. Though acknowledging the existence of new types of problems, few authors have been willing to push aside war, peace, security, and order for other priorities. Paradigmatic consensus persists, though not unchallenged. Why is this the case?

There are numerous explanations no doubt, but the human's propensity to study pathology, whether in medicine, journalism, or international relations, is surely an important one. Journalists do not report "nonevents." Conflict, catastrophe, scandal, crime, and vice always precede achievement because they are assumed to be deviations from the norm. Likewise, medical research seldom focuses on the healthy person. And so, faced with the cataclysmic and sudden possibilty of war anywhere on the earth, international politics and theory as fields of inquiry have always revolved around this problem. Not even proponents of the war-is-inevitable school, such as Lenin, lost interest in the phenomenon just because it was recurring.

In contrast, population problems, resource depletion, environmental degradation appear only slowly in our awareness, and do not bear the immediate costs and destruction associated with violence between states. The global problems favored by the WOMP group make good documentaries, but not daily television fare, such as a war does. In other words, war has an immediacy and a magnitude of costs and tragedy associated with it that are not shared by other problematics.

The study of peaceful—normal—relations has never commanded much attention in the field, probably for reasons similar to journalists' emphasis on the spectacular and deviant. Nothing can put a European international politics audience to sleep faster than a lecture on Canadian-American relations, or for a North American audience a seminar on intra-Scandinavian cooperation in communications and welfare policies. This is also a problem confronting those who would put transnational relationships at the forefront of inquiry. The regular, the routine, the mundane taken by themselves fail to have an intrinsic interest except for a few specialists. But if those studies can be linked to the traditional problematic, as integration theorists have done, then they immediately take on greater intrinsic *and* theoretical interest.

International politics and theory as fields of teaching and research face numerous problems. The consensus on core questions has broken down to be replaced by a diversity that is sometimes disturbing (even though the diversity is not yet strongly reflected in textbooks). We have courses and sections of courses dealing with international politics, world politics, international relations, strategic studies, peace science, conflict resolution, peace studies, international political economy, international law and organization, world modeling, and no doubt courses dealing with some of the plethora of problems on the global agenda. Such an array can only be bewildering to students, future scholars in the field, teachers of courses, and those who engage in research. The volume of literature in all these subfields combined is already too large for any single person to keep up with, much less to summarize in a semester course. Whether in teaching or research, then, the growing diversity in the field requires choices, and therefore some guidelines for priorities.

This discussion has been designed to assist those who are having difficulties making those choices. To put the conclusion succinctly: the classical paradigm provides a core for both descriptive and theoretical efforts. It can accommodate new types of actors and issues, and with some imaginative theorizing, it can incorporate some of the insights emerging from the challenging paradigms. The case that the classical paradigm is obsolete has not been made, persuasively, on either theoretical or empirical grounds. Many of the criticisms are, in fact, based on erroneous or incomplete characterizations of it. If the theoretical core—the essential characteristics of a states system and the problematic—is ignored, downplayed, or dismissed as irrelevant, then the field will fly apart into ghettoes of specialization, and international theory will exist only as an unlinked group of micro and middle-range generalizations, often reflecting current issues of the day or the latest intellectual fad. The degree of paradigmatic orthodoxy reported in Chapter 5 is not, then, a matter of concern, but on the contrary demonstrates that most practitioners in the field know what is central to the discipline, and what is of subsidiary or peripheral theoretical importance. Yet the challenging paradigms are becoming more visible, and at the level of research and professional communication, they are commanding much more than passing attention.

Enhancing Mutual Awareness

While there are reasons for applauding paradigmatic paramountcy (but not theoretical stagnation), the portrait of scholarly communication between national academic communities is a cause for some concern. The concern is that a field of inquiry which seems to have intrinsic importance from a scientific, theoretical, and normative point of view, is limited to only a few countries. One has the feeling, in describing the debates about paradigms, that outside of a few anglophone countries, no one really cares. To others, perhaps, the problems discussed in this and many other volumes may appear as only the domestic quarrels of a small cult.

But the proliferation of courses, research institutes, and

publications on international relations in many countries suggests that this is not the case. There is a latent community of scholars doing work in international politics and theory, and it is difficult to believe that many of them do not have to make difficult choices as well. The problem is that the community is latent; the pattern of scholarly exchange is such that a core generates the vast majority of work in international theory, peripheries "consume" that work, but the core remains very poorly informed about the activities of scholars in the peripheries. The figures in the preceding chapter do not suggest that this picture is changing; on the contrary, for most countries in our sample, the trend is toward greater intellectual self-reliance and parochialism. There is only a single important exception to this proposition. Dependency theory, despite its Marxist roots, is essentially an intellectual creation of the Third World, probably the first systematic set of statements about international relations dynamics to emerge from an area outside Europe and North America. It has been "consumed" eagerly (if not always comprehendingly) in the center; it has stimulated research, proliferation of "schools," research institutes, journals, and the like. But dependency theory is unique in this sense; no similar theories have emerged from other peripheries.

Some may claim that there is no intrinsic problem in continuing the Anglo-American intellectual condominium, that when quality work is done anywhere, it will eventually enter the web of communications. The tendencies reported in the previous chapter represent the conscious choices of textbook authors, and as in a free market, those ideas, concepts, innovations, paradigms, and data sets that reflect the highest quality, will gain their due recognition. Since obviously there is no conspiracy to limit membership in the international theory club, merit is the only criterion for mutual acknowledgment. The "producers" of today will "consume" work from abroad when and if it meets certain scholarly standards, as well as the standards of the field: namely, that these must be theories of international relations, and not merely analyses of various countries' foreign policy problems, current affairs reporting, or analysis of passing regional problems.

There is merit to this view and it is probably a sufficient explanation for the communications profile of the community until recently. But today there is an inverse relationship between the institutionalized growth of international relations and theory in the peripheries and Europe on the one hand, and the

145

trend toward greater reliance on national literatures on the other. The slight increase in acknowledgment of works by Canadian, Australian, and Third World authors is outdistanced by English and American self-references, which have reached magnitudes approaching 90 percent.

Why should such trends cause concern as long as high quality work is being published somewhere? Isn't the ideal of an international community of scholars unattainable as long as academic resources are distributed so unevenly in the world? There are at least two answers. First, despite the great intellectual contributions made by the fathers of the classical tradition, and all of their modern successors, the tradition has been based on the European and cold war historical experiences. There are bound to be biases, omissions, and lacunae. Dependency theories have demonstrated that certain classes of states face sets of problems that neither the historical European states experienced, nor that present-day industrial nations either confront or fully comprehend. Whether or not one accepts those theories as reasonable explanations of historical processes, they do contain important generalizations about industrial state-developing state relations that were of no concern to Hobbes, Rousseau, the nineteenth-century liberals, and most twentieth-century successors. It would be short-sighted in the extreme to believe that past and present formulations in international theory have posed or answered all the key questions for all sorts of states with highly diversified historical experiences.

Even the critics of the classical states system paradigm, particularly those who promote the study of transnational relations, as well as certain writers in the WOMP tradition, display strong biases toward the problems and processes typical of relations only between industrial states. To talk of global interdependence, the profusion of INGOs, or global problems such as ecological degradation is to overlook the fact that a majority of the new states are not interdependent in any sense of the word that implies reasonable symmetry in relationships, that they barely participate at all in INGO activity, and that they contribute virtually nothing to "global" ecological problems. Modern writers have, in their enthusiasm for globalism, unwittingly attributed to all states in the system the characteristics which are only typical of the handful of industrial countries. The vast differences between states, along numerous dimensions, are systematically ignored in most versions of international theory. For a variety of sociological reasons (for example, how many theorists have actually resided in a developing country for a significant period of time?) these types of biases and short-comings are not likely to be corrected or filled in by scholars from the Anglo-American condominium—or from some of the peripheral countries studied here, for that matter. My bet is that a reasonably isomorphic model of international politics will not emerge until scholars from many types of societies have contributed to it.

The second answer to the questions is that many, perhaps most, authors do not seek to reach international audiences, and thereby deprive those elsewhere who might be interested in ideas, new approaches, methodological innovations, and old-fashioned insights. The patterns of scholarship in most countries remain parochial not because authors in some countries "dominate" the field, or because certain clubs exclude those with improper credentials, but because the scholars themselves do not regularly seek to have their ideas enter the network of scholarly communication. The unseen audience to whom they are writing is usually a national one. Takashi Inoguchi has summarized the situation in Japan; it is probably a good description of scholarship in most countries today:

> Japanese political scientists are still parochial in the sense that they do not pay much attention to how their works are related to works on the world's frontiers of knowledge and how they could contribute to the world intellectual community. They tend to pay almost exclusive attention to the Japanese audience, whether highly specialized or more general. [Part of the problem is due to language.] It is also due to the fact that Japanese political scientists have a huge domestic market for their writings, which are thus often tailored to the preference of the general audience, most importantly white collar employees, businessmen, and bureaucrats as well as students. (Inoguchi 1982, 209)

While Inoguchi's description refers to political science, the position of Japanese scholars specializing in international relations is not significantly different. If anything, however, we would expect differences between political science and international relations. Most political scientists are working in areas related to national politics. These are often of little interest to their colleagues in other countries, except area specialists and those in comparative politics whose interests expand beyond the traditional great powers. In contrast, international theory is concerned with phenomena, structures, and processes that impinge on many other countries, and should therefore appeal to an international audience. Yet the figures in the preceding chapter are similar to studies made recently on citation patterns in political science generally. For example, an article published in 1977 reported that of the American, British, Canadian, and Indian journal authorships, the average percentage of references to national colleagues was 82.2, with the United States most self-reliant at 90.7 percent. Another study of three American journals, in 1968–9, revealed that on average 82.3 percent of all the articles had not a single reference to a work in a foreign language (Hajjar et al. 1977; Pfotenhauer 1972, as summarized in Gareau 1981, 783–4). Overall the trend is toward greater insularity in political science. These figures are significant not only because they are so similar to those reported in Chapter 6, but also because they refer to the patterns of citation in the main media of scholarly exchange—journal articles—and not to textbooks. The objection that texts are not a good indicator of the flow of communications at the professional level must thus be set aside.

The available evidence thus strongly supports a conclusion that patterns of international exchange of scholarly knowledge in our field remain far from an ideal model of an international community of scholars, and that over time parochialism in reading habits, publication for national audiences, and mutual reference is increasing. The two answers outlined above provide part of the explanation of the puzzle, but surely not all of it. Other factors such as translation, the structure of the publishing industry, the need to develop a scholarly reputation among national colleagues for career advancement, and the like, are no doubt also relevant. But the contradiction remains: as the institutional mechanisms for reasonably symmetrical or proportional communication have developed, the scholarly enterprise in international theory has become less international.

The problem cannot be solved by preaching a type of global academic brotherhood. But an enhanced awareness of the problem might help to reverse present trends. In the meantime, exciting developments in a revived field of international theory must be assessed soberly in the knowledge that perhaps all the insights, wisdom, knowledge, and intellectually attractive ideas of the classical tradition, and of the modern challengers, are incomplete until more scholars interpreting a variety of

historical experiences have had their opportunity to contribute
to the field.

Notes: Chapter 7

1 I have made the same point in reviewing the Keohane—Nye volume, *Power
and Interdependence* (Holsti 1978: 525).
2 A more recent study of the effects of increased interdependence on foreign
policy-making organizations in Norway found few of the anticipated
changes. The five main characteristics of interdependence: (1) a greater
number and more diffuse issues; (2) the domination of the agenda by
economic issues; (3) erosion of the foreign–domestic policy distinction; (4)
the involvement of new types of actors; and (5) some loss of control and coordination of foreign policy by the foreign ministry. The only significant
development predicted by increased interdependence was the growth of the
number of Norway's diplomatic missions abroad, and the enlargement of
some bureaux in the foreign policy machinery in Oslo. Note, however, that
the numerical growth of people involved in the formulation and execution of
policy can be accounted for just as well by the *increased number of states in the
system* with which Norway has established diplomatic relations. See East and
Salomonson 1981.
3 For case studies of autonomy-enhancing foreign policy, see Holsti et al. 1980a.

Appendix

Table A-1 *Authors and Texts, United States*

Authors	Title	Year	No. of Refs
1. H. J. Morgenthau	*Politics among Nations*	1948	317
2. R. Strausz-Hupé and S. Possony	*International Relations in the Age of Conflict between Democracy and Dictatorship*	1950	279[a]
3. N. Palmer and H. C. Perkins	*International Relations, 2nd ed.*	1957	334[b]
4. N. D. Hill	*International Politics*	1963	319[c]
5. V. Van Dyke	*International Politics, 2nd ed.*	1966	313
6. A. F. K. Organski	*World Politics, 2nd ed.*	1968	331
7. W. D. Coplin	*Introduction to International Politics*	1974	512
8. R. Sterling	*Macropolitics: International Relations in a Global Society*	1974	147
9. K. W. Deutsch	*The Analysis of International Relations, 2nd ed.*	1978	285
10. J. L. Ray	*Global Politics*	1979	321
11. B. Russett and H. Starr	*World Politics: The Menu for Choice*	1981	352
12. C. W. Kegley and E. Wittkopf	*World Politics: Trends and Transformation*	1981	492

[a]Excludes references to chs. 11, 13, 16–19, 22–5, 29.
[b]Excludes references to chs. 14–24.
[c]Excludes references to ch. 3.

Table A-2 *Authors and Texts, Great Britain*

Authors	Title	Year	No. of Refs
1. G. Schwarzenberger	*Power Politics*, 2nd ed.	1951	412
2. W. Friedmann	*Introduction to World Politics*	1951	46
3. J. Burton	*International Relations: A General Theory*	1965	72
4. J. Burton	*Systems, States, Diplomacy, Rules*	1968	62
5. J. Frankel	*International Relations, 2nd ed.*	1969	26
6. F. S. Northedge and M. J. Grieve	*A Hundred Years of International Relations*	1971	121
7. J. Burton	*World Society*	1972	41[a]
8. J. Frankel	*Contemporary Theory and the Behaviour of States*	1973	73
9. C. Reynolds	*Theory and Explanation in International Politics*	1973	121
10. F. S. Northedge	*The International Political System*	1976	78
11. H. Bull	*The Anarchical Society*	1977	119
12. J. Frankel	*International Relations in a Changing World*	1979	27
13. P. A. Reynolds	*An Introduction to International Relations*	1980	44

[a]Footnotes only.

Table A-3 *Authors and Texts, Korea*

Authors	Title	Year	No. of Refs
1. Lee Yong-Hee	*General Theories of International Relations*	1962	158[a]
2. Choi Jong-Kie	*International Relations*	1966	216
3. Lee Kie-Won	"A study of power in International Relations"	1970	17[a]
4. Kim Hak-Joon	"Two conflicting aspects of the modern 'State of War'"	1972	29[a]
5. Cho Jae-Kwan	*International Politics, 2nd ed.*	1976	131
6. Kim Sang-Joon	*Theories of International Politics*	1977	73
7. Rhee Sang-Woo	*Contemporary Theories in International Relations*	1979	40
8. Kim Sang-Joon	*Theories of International Politics, II*	1980	143
9. Park Sang-Shik	*International Politics*	1981	143
10. Oh Kie-Pyung	*The Politics of International Organizations: Task Systems in International Relations*	1982	167

[a]Footnotes only.

Table A-4 *Authors and Texts, India*

Authors	Title	Year	No. of Refs
1. D. S. Sangha	*Rise of the New Asia*	1948	138
2. K. P. Karunakaran	*India in World Affairs*	1958	108
3. S. Gupta	*India and Regional Integration in Asia*	1964	76
4. A. Appadorai	*Essays in Politics and International Relations*	1969	112[a]
5. A. H. Doctor	*International Relations: An Introductory Study*	1969	100
6. M. S. Rajan	*Non-Alignment; India and the Future*	1970	18
7. R. Chakravarti	*International Relations*	1970	277
8. M. Kumar	*Violence and Non-Violence in International Relations*	1975	193
9. S. Chawla	*The Foreign Relations of India*	1976	66[a]
10. A. P. Rana	*The Imperatives of Nonalignment*	1976	366
11. K. P. Misra	*Quest for an International Order in the Indian Ocean*	1977	138
12. P. K. Misra	*India, Pakistan, Nepal and Bangladesh*	1979	166
13. L. P. Singh	*India's Foreign Policy*	1980	162

[a]Footnotes only.

Table A-5 *Authors and Texts, France*

Authors	Title	Year	No. of Refs
1. R. Aron	*Paix et guerre: théorie des relations internationales*	1966	105[a]
2. P. Renouvin and J. B. Duroselle	*Introduction to the History of International Relations*	1967	298
3. M. Merle	*Sociologie des relations internationales*	1974	133[a]

[a]Footnotes only.

Table A-6 *Authors and Texts, Canada and Australia*

Authors	Title	Year	No. of Refs
1. A. L. Burns	*Of Powers and their Politics*	1968	49[a]
2. W. A. Axline and J. A. Stegenga[b]	*The Global Community: A Brief Introduction to International Relations*	1972	34
3. C. Pentland	*International Theory and European Integration*	1973	263[a]
4. R. Pettman	*Human Behaviour and World Politics: An Introduction to International Relations*	1975	333
5. R. Pettman	*State and Class: A Sociology of International Affairs*	1979	354[a]
6. I. Clark	*Reform and Resistance in the International Order*	1980	121[a]
7. J. D. B. Miller	*The World of States*	1981	73[a]
8. K. J. Holsti	*International Politics, 4th ed.*	1983	471

[a]Footnotes only.
[b]Senior author is Canadian, co-author is American

Table A-7 *Authors and Texts, Japan*

Authors	Title	Date
1. H. Kamikawa	Kokusaiseijigaku-gairon (International Politics)	1950[a]
2. M. Uchiyama	Kokusaiseijigaku-josetsu (Introduction to International Politics)	1953[a]
3. T. Kawata	Kokusaikankei-gairon (International Relations)	1958[a]
4. K. Mushakoji and M. Royama	Kokusaiseiji-gaku (International Politics)	1976
5. K. Mushakoji and M. Royama	Kokusai-gaku (International Studies)	1976
6. H. Hanai	Kokusaikankei-ron (International Relations)	1980[b]
7. S. Eto et al.	Kokusaikankei-ron (International Relations)	1980
8. H. Seki	Kokusaiseijigaku o manabu (The Study of International Politics)	1981
9. S. Matsumoto et al.	Kokusaiseiji (International Politics)	1981
10. N. Tanaka	Kokusaikankei-ron (International Relations)	1981
11. T. Saito	Kokusaikankeiron-nyûmon (Introduction to International Relations)	1981
12. C. Hosoya et al.	Kokusaiseiji no sekai (The World of International Politics)	1981[a]

[a]Only footnotes used.
[b]Footnotes and "suggested readings" used together.

Table B-1 *Nationalities of Authors Cited in References for this Volume*

Country/Region	Number	Percent
United States	56	49.6
Great Britain	21	18.6
Canada	8	7.0
Europe	7	6.2
Australia	7	6.2
Scandinavia	5	4.4
Latin America	4	3.5
Communist	1	0.9
Japan	1	0.9
India	1	0.9
Africa	1	0.9
Unknown	1	0.9
	113	100.0

References

Amstrop, Nils. 1978. "The 'early' Morgenthau: a comment on the intellectual origins of realism." *Conflict and Cooperation* 13:163–75.

Aron, Raymond. 1966. *War and Peace: A Theory of International Relations.* Translated by Annette Baker Fox. New York: Praeger.

Baran, Paul. 1957. *The Political Economy of Growth.* New York: Monthly Review Press.

Beitz, Charles R. 1979. *Political Theory and International Relations.* Princeton, N.J.: Princeton University Press.

Bentham, Jeremy. 1974. "Plan for Universal and Perpetual Peace." *Peace Projects of the Eighteenth Century.* Edited by M. C. Jacob. New York: Garland.

Beres, Louise René, and Harry Targ, eds. 1975. *Planning Alternative Futures.* New York: Praeger.

Brewer, Anthony. 1980. *Marxist Theories of Imperialism: A Critical Survey.* London: Routledge & Kegan Paul.

Brown, Lester. 1972. *World without Borders.* New York: Random House.

Bull, Hedley. 1966. "Grotian conceptions of international society." In *Diplomatic Investigations.* See Butterfield and Wight 1966.

Bull, Hedley. 1977. *The Anarchical Society.* London: Macmillan.

Burton, John. 1972. *World Society.* Cambridge: Cambridge University Press.

Butterfield, Herbert, and Martin Wight, eds. 1966. *Diplomatic Investigations: Essays in the Theory of International Politics.* London: Allen & Unwin.

Cardoso, Fernando. 1977. "The consumption of dependency theory in the United States." *Latin American Research Review* 12: 7–24.

Cardoso, Fernando, and Enzo Faletto. 1979. *Dependency and Development in Latin America.* Translated by M. M. Urquidi. Berkeley, Calif.: University of California Press.

Chase-Dunn, Christopher. 1979. "Comparative research on world system characteristics." *International Studies Quarterly* 23 (December): 601–23.

Chase-Dunn, Christopher. 1981. "Interstate system and capitalist world-economy: one logic or two?" *International Studies Quarterly* 25 (March): 19–42.

Clark, Grenville, and Louis B. Sohn. 1962. *World Peace through World Law.* 2nd ed. Cambridge, Mass.: Harvard University Press.

Clark, Ian. 1980. *Reform and Resistance in the International Order.* Cambridge: Cambridge University Press.

Collins, Hugh. 1982. "Problems of a fragmented field." *Academic Studies and International Politics*. Edited by Coral Bell. Canberra Studies in World Affairs, no. 6. Canberra: Australian National University.

Crucé, Emeric. 1972. *The New Cineas*. Translated by C. Frederick Farrell, Jr., and Edith R. Farrell. New York: Garland.

de Callières, François. 1716. *De la manière de négocier avec les souverains*. Paris: Mercure Gallant.

Deutsch, Karl, et al. 1977. *Problems of World Modeling*. Cambridge, Mass.: Ballinger.

Donelan, Michael, ed. 1978. *The Reason of States: A Study in International Political Theory*. London: Allen & Unwin.

Doran, Charles F. 1983. "War and power dynamics: economic underpinnings." *International Studies Quarterly* 27 (December): 419–42.

East, Maurice, and Leif-Helge Salomonson. 1981. "Adapting foreign policy making to interdependence: a proposal and some evidence from Norway." *Conflict and Cooperation* 16: 165–82.

Falk, Richard A. 1971. *This Endangered Planet*. New York: Random House.

Falk, Richard A. 1977. "Contending approaches to world order." *Journal of International Affairs* 31 (Fall/Winter): 171–98.

Frank, André Gunder. 1972. "The development of underdevelopment." In *Dependence and Under-Development*, by James Cockcroft, André Gunder Frank, and Dale L. Johnson. New York: Doubleday.

Gallie, W. B. 1978. *Philosophers of Peace and War: Kant, Clausewitz, Engels and Tolstoy*. Cambridge: Cambridge University Press.

Galtung, Johan. 1971. "A structural theory of imperialism." *Journal of Peace Research* 8: 81–117.

Galtung, Johan. 1980. *The True Worlds: A Transnational Perspective*. New York: The Free Press.

Gareau, Frederick H. 1981. "The discipline international relations: a multinational perspective." *Journal of Politics* 43 (August): 779–802.

Gierke, Otto von. 1955. *Johannes Althusius und die Entwicklung der naturrechtlichen staatstheorien*. Aslen: Scientia.

Gilpin, Robert. 1981. *War and Change in World Politics*. Cambridge: Cambridge University Press.

Grotius, Hugo. 1925. *De jure belli et pacis*. London: Oxford University Press.

Hajjar, Sami G., et al. 1977. "The literature of political science: professional journals in four nations." *International Social Science Journal* 29: 327–32.

Hinsley, F. H. 1967. *Power and the Pursuit of Peace*. Cambridge: Cambridge University Press.

Hinsley, F. H. 1981. *The Fall and Rise of the Modern International System*. The Arthur Yencken Memorial Lecture, 1980. Canberra Studies in World Affairs, no. 4. Canberra: Australian National University.

Hobbes, Thomas. 1651. *Leviathan*. London: Andrew Crooke.

Hoffmann, Stanley. 1965. *The State of War: Essays on the Theory and Practice of International Relations*. New York: Praeger.

Hoffmann, Stanley. 1978. *Primacy or World Order: American Foreign Policy since the Cold War*. New York: McGraw-Hill.

REFERENCES

Holsti, K. J. 1971. "Retreat from Utopia: international relations theory, 1945–1970." *Canadian Journal of Political Science* 4: 165–77.

Holsti, K. J. 1975. "Underdevelopment and the 'gap' theory of international conflict." *American Political Science Review* 69 (September): 827–39.

Holsti, K. J. 1978. "A new international politics? Diplomacy in complex interdependence." *International Organization* 32 (Spring): 513–30.

Holsti, K. J. 1980a. "Change in the international system: integration and fragmentation." In *Change in the International System*, edited by Ole R. Holsti, Randolph Siverson, and Alexander George. Boulder, Colo.: Westview Press.

Holsti, K. J. 1980b. "Detente and peaceful co-existence: assessing the possibilities." *Co-Existence* 17 (April): 1–19.

Holsti, K. J. 1982. *Why Nations Realign: Foreign Policy Restructuring in the Postwar World*. London: Allen & Unwin.

Inkeles, Alex. 1975. "The emerging social structure of the world." *World Politics* 27 (July): 467–95.

Inkeles, Alex. 1981. "Convergence and divergence in industrial societies." In *Directions of Change: Modernization Theory, Research, and Realities*. by Mustafa Attir et al. Boulder, Colo.: Westview Press.

Inoguchi, Takashi. 1982. "Japan." In *International Handbook of Political Science*. Edited by William G. Andrews. Westport, Conn.: Greenwood Press.

Kant, Immanuel. 1957. *Perpetual Peace*. Edited by Lewis White Beck. New York: Bobbs-Merrill.

Kaplan, Morton. 1957. *System and Process in International Politics*. New York: Wiley.

Kent, R. C., and G. P. Nicholson, eds. 1980. *The Study and Teaching of International Relations*. New York: Nichols.

Keohane, Robert, and Joseph S. Nye, Jr., eds. 1972. *World Politics and Transnational Relations*. Cambridge, Mass.: Harvard University Press.

Keohane, Robert, and Joseph S. Nye, Jr. 1977. *Power and Interdependence*. Boston, Mass.: Little, Brown.

Kothari, Rajni. 1974. *Footsteps into the Future*. New York: The Free Press.

Krasner, Stephen. 1978. *Defending the National Interest: Raw Materials, Investments and U.S. Foreign Policy*. Princeton, N.J.: Princeton University Press.

Kuhn, Thomas. 1962. *The Structure of Scientific Revolutions*: Chicago: University of Chicago Press.

Kulbakova, V., and A. A. Cruickshank. 1980. *Marxism-Leninism and Theory of International Relations*. London: Routledge & Kegan Paul.

La Barr, Dorothy F., and J. David Singer. 1976. *The Study of International Politics: A Guide to the Sources for the Student, Teacher, and Researcher*. Santa Barbara, Calif.: Clio Books.

Lenin. 1939. *Imperialism, the Highest Stage of Capitalism*. New York. International Publishers.

Lijphart, Arend. 1974. "The structure of the theoretical revolution in international relations." *International Studies Quarterly* 18 (March): 41–74.

159

Little, Richard. 1978. "A systems approach." In *Approaches and Theory in International Relations*. *See* Taylor 1978a.

McGowan, Patrick, and Stephen B. Walker. 1981. "Radical and conventional models of U.S. foreign economic policy making." *World Politics* 33 (August): 347–83.

Mansbach, Richard, and John Vasquez. 1981. *In Search of Theory: A New Paradigm for Global Politics*. New York: Columbia University Press.

Maghroori, Ray, and Bennett Ramberg. 1982. *Globalism versus Realism: International Relations' Third Debate*. Boulder, Colo.: Westview Press.

Mazrui, Ali. 1981. "Micro-dependency: the Cuban factor in Southern Africa." *India Quarterly* 37 (July–September): 329–45.

Mendlowitz, Saul H. 1977. "The program of the Institute of World Order." *Journal of International Affairs* 31 (Fall/Winter): 259–66.

Miller, J. D. B. 1981. *The World of States*. London: Croom Helm.

Mische, Gerald, and Patricia Mische. 1977. *Toward a Human World Order*. New York: Paulist Press.

Mitchell, C. R. 1980. "Analyzing the 'great debates': teaching methodology in a decade of change." In *The Study and Teaching of International Relations*. *See* Kent and Nicholson 1980.

Morse, Edward. 1976. *Modernization and the Transformation of International Relations*. New York: The Free Press.

Navari, Cornelia. 1978. "Knowledge, the state and the state of nature." In *The Reason of States*. *See* Donelan 1978.

Nye, Joseph S., Jr. 1976. "Transnational relations and interstate conflicts: an empirical analysis." In *Canada and the United States: Transnational and Transgovernmental Relations*, by Annette B. Fox, Alfred O. Hero, Jr., and Joseph S. Nye. New York: Columbia University Press.

Parkinson, F. 1977. *The Philosophy of International Relations: A Study in the History of Thought*. Beverly Hills, Calif.: Sage Publications.

Pentland, Charles. 1973. *International Theory and European Integration*. New York: Praeger.

Pettman, Ralph. 1979. *State and Class: A Sociology of International Affairs*. London: Croom Helm.

Pfotenhauer, David. 1972. "Conceptions of political science in Western Germany and the United States, 1960–1969." *Journal of Politics* 34: 554–91.

Puchala, Donald, and Stuart Fagan. 1974. "International politics in the 1970s: the search for a perspective." *International Organization* 28 (Spring): 247–66.

Reynolds, Charles. 1981. *Modes of Imperialism*. Oxford: Martin Robertson.

Rosecrance, Richard. 1963. *Action and Reaction in International Politics*. Boston: Little, Brown.

Rosenau, James. 1980. *The Study of Global Interdependence*. London: Pinter.

Rousseau, Jean-Jacques. n.d. *A Lasting Peace through the Federation of Europe*. Translated by C. E. Vaughan. New Haven, Conn.: Whitloch.

Rummel, Rudolph J. 1983. "Libertarianism and international violence." *Journal of Conflict Resolution* 77 (March): 27–72.

REFERENCES

Russell, Frank M. 1936. *Theories of International Relations*. New York: Appleton-Century.

Saint-Pierre, Charles Castel de. 1927. *Extrait du projet de paix perpetuelle*. London: R. Cobden-Sanderson.

Savigear, P. 1978. "European political philosophy and the theory of international relations." In *Approaches and Theory in International Relations*. See Taylor 1978a.

Scott, Andrew M. 1982. *The Dynamics of Interdependence*. Chapel Hill, N.C.: University of North Carolina Press.

Spiro, Herbert J. 1966. *World Politics: The Global System*. Homewood, Ill.: Dorsey Press.

Sprout, Harold, and Margaret Sprout. 1971. *Towards a Politics of the Planet Earth*. New York: van Nostrand.

Sullivan, Michael. 1982. "The realities of the present system." In *Globalism versus Realism*. See Maghroori and Ramberg 1982.

Taylor, Trevor, ed. 1978a. *Approaches and Theory in International Relations*. London: Longman.

Taylor, Trevor. 1978b. "Power politics." In *Approaches and Theory in International Relations*. See Taylor 1978a.

Thorndike, Tony. 1978. "The revolutionary approach: the Marxist perspective." In *Approaches and Theory in International Relations*. See Taylor 1978a.

Tooze, Roger. 1981. "Economics, international political economy and change in the international system." In *Change and the Study of International Relations: The Evaded Dimension*, edited by Barry Buzan and R. J. Barry Jones. London: Pinter.

Väyrynen, Raimo. 1983. "Economic cycles, power transitions, political management and wars between major powers." *International Studies Quarterly* 27 (December): 389–418.

Vollerthun, Ursula. n.d. "The idea of international society: a study of the 'via media' tradition in the theory of international relations." Ph.D. thesis, Department of International Relations, Australian National University.

Wallerstein, Immanuel. 1974. *The Modern World-System*. New York: Academic Press.

Wallerstein, Immanuel. 1979. *The Capitalist World Economy*. Cambridge and Paris: Cambridge University Press and Editions de la Maison des Sciences de L'Homme.

Waltz, Kenneth. 1959. *Man, the State, and War*. New York: Columbia University Press.

Waltz, Kenneth. 1979. *Theory of International Politics*. Reading, Mass.: Addison-Wesley.

Wesson, Robert G. 1978. *State Systems: International Pluralism, Politics, and Culture*. New York: The Free Press.

Wight, Martin. 1966a. "Western values in international relations." In *Diplomatic Investigations*. See Butterfield and Wight 1966.

Wight, Martin. 1966b. "Why is there no international theory?" In *Diplomatic Investigations*. See Butterfield and Wight 1966.

Willetts, Peter. 1981. "The United Nations and the transformation of the interstate system." In *Change and the Study of International Relations: The Evaded Dimension*, edited by Barry Buzan and R. J. Barry Jones. London: Pinter.

Zolberg, Aristide R. 1981. "Origins of the modern world system: a missing link." *World Politics* 33 (January): 253–81.

Index